SHADOWS OF ECSTASY & RUMOURS OF GLORY

THE INFLUENCE OF CHARLES WILLIAMS ON THE SONGWRITING OF BRUCE COCKBURN

JOHN R. MABRY

APOCRYPHILE PRESS

Apocryphile Press
PO Box 255
Hannacroix, NY 12087
www.apocryphilepress.com

Printed in the United States of America
ISBN 978-1-965646-70-0 | paper
ISBN 978-1-965646-71-7 | ePub

CONTENTS

ACKNOWLEDGMENTS

This began as an article...and then it just kept growing. But I had to stop somewhere. For each point, I may give one or two examples from Cockburn's portfolio. There may be many more, but I don't want to overtax the reader with these. Please know that this is a far from exhaustive treatment, and there is more to be done on the topic.

Throughout, page numbers for Williams' novels are given using the Apocryphile Press editions, although the pagination is not far off from the Eerdman's editions most people in the United States are familiar with. I am grateful to those Williams scholars who contributed new introductions to the Apocryphile editions: Edward Gauntlett, Gwendolen Grant, Sørina Higgins, Grevel Lindop, and Aren Roukema. The epigraph from the Gospel of Philip that opens Part II is from my own version.

Special thanks are due to Bruce Hunter, executor of the Williams estate for his kind permission to use the many quotations from CW's writings. Equal gratitude is due to Bernie Finkelstein, Bruce Cockburn's manager and Round Hill Carlin for graciously granting permission to quote Cockburn's lyrics.

I am grateful to The Cockburn Project (https://cockburnproject.net/) for their vast library of Cockburn lyrics, complete with every statement Cockburn has given as to the meaning behind each lyric, both in public statements and in private.

Many thanks to Sørina Higgins, who encouraged me in this research and offered her The Oddest Inkling blog as a suitable vehicle for publication...until it got too long for that.

I also want to thank my editor, Dr. Janeen Jones, for putting the polish on this pearl. Thanks to Bob Hudson for being one of those rare souls who was already familiar with both Williams and Cockburn and for his lovely and humbling foreword. And thanks to Fr. Daniel Keebler (keeper of the Gavin's Woodpile website, celebrating all things Cockburn) and Kevin Kelly for their kind permission to use their photos of Bruce.

Finally, a big thank you to my wife, who listened to drafts of this as I read them aloud to her, and for her loving and supportive course corrections. And thanks to the wider community of Inklings scholars, who have welcomed me to their Festival of Friends.

ABBREVIATIONS USED

CHARLES WILLIAMS' NOVELS

AHE / All Hallows' Eve
DiH / Descent into Hell
GT / The Greater Trumps
MD / Many Dimensions
PL / The Place of the Lion
SoE / Shadows of Ecstasy
WiH / War in Heaven

BRUCE COCKBURN'S ALBUMS

AAA / Anything Anytime Anywhere (2002)
BC / Bruce Cockburn (eponymous; 1970)
BiC / Big Circumstance (1988)
BoB / Bone on Bone (2017)
BNO / Breakfast in New Orleans, Dinner in Timbuktu (1999)
CoN / The Charity of Night (1996)
D2H / Dart to the Heart (1994)
DDJ / Dancing in the Dragon's Jaws (1979)

FAO / Further Adventures Of (1978)
HU / Humans (1980)
HWWS / High Winds, White Sky (1971)
IFD / In the Falling Dark (1976)
ICF / Inner City Front (1981)
LSCN / Life Short, Call Now (2006)
MD / Mummy Dust (compilation; 1981)
NBBL / Nothing But a Burning Light (1991)
OSOM / Oh Sun, Oh Moon (2023)
SF / Stealing Fire (1984)
SOL / Slice O Life: Live Solo (2009)
SST / Salt, Sun & Time (1974)
TwN / The Trouble with Normal (1983)
WoW / World of Wonders (1986)
YNSE / You've Never Seen Everything (2003)

FOREWORD

FESTIVAL OF FRIENDS

BY ROBERT HUDSON

You'd be hard-pressed to find a Christian bookstore today that stocks both the writings of Charles Williams and the recordings of Bruce Cockburn (which may tell you something about the state of our current culture), and yet it was my good fortune in the winter of 1979/80 to work as a clerk in just such a bookstore in Chapel Hill, North Carolina, and, in my memory at least, I discovered both artists at nearly the same moment.

Before then, I was familiar with Cockburn's song "One Day I Walk" and found it intriguing, but then, like many other music fans, I fell in love with his "Wondering Where the Lions Are," which was beginning to get radio airplay that winter. The song was the Canadian musician's breakthrough hit in the US market, and so popular did it become that he was invited to be a musical guest on *Saturday Night Live* the following May (where he was paired, somewhat oddly, with country rockers the Amazing Rhythm Aces).

The Christian themes woven throughout Cockburn's album *Dancing in the Dragon's Jaws*, on which "Wondering Where the Lions Are" appears, earned it a slot in the vinyl-record bins of the store I worked in. I would pipe it through the store's sound system in rotation with albums by Amy Grant, Barry McGuire,

Keith Green, Larry Norman, and, of course, Bob Dylan's *Slow Train Coming*, which was 1979's surprise love-it-or-hate-it gift to the Christian faithful (I loved it, of course, and still do), but while I was sometimes asked to take Dylan off the turntable, no one ever objected to Cockburn.

Over that Christmas break, with Cockburn's song still ringing in my ears, I read Williams's novel *The Place of the Lion* and, for the first time, C. S. Lewis's *The Lion, the Witch and the Wardrobe* —a veritable pride of lions converging in a literary savannah. Clearly, something was up, some esoteric connection existed, leaving me with only the vaguest notion of what *lion*, as a concept, might mean to them. With more reading and more listening I came to appreciate the contours of those connections —the Platonist imagery of a lion-beyond-all-lions, of the ideal forms of which our material world is but a faint shadow, of higher realities ready to burst like solar flares into our day-to-day lives.

But it was not until this past month, while reading Rev. Dr. John R. Mabry's *Shadows of Ecstasy and Rumours of Glory*, that I realized how profound those connections truly are—and how *many* more connections exist that I've never even imagined. As I discovered influence upon influence, I was fascinated, and if you, reader, are even the least bit acquainted with the writings of Charles Williams and the music of Bruce Cockburn, I know you will be fascinated as well.

Cockburn's eyes and ears were open to a host of other influences besides Williams, poets in particular: T. S. Eliot, Blaise Cendrars, Ernesto Cardenal, Allen Ginsberg and the Beats, François Villon, Al Purdy, Robert Graves, Pablo Neruda, and many more. And lest we forget his guitar playing, Cockburn absorbed and adapted the stylings of blues players like Mississippi John Hurt and John Lee Hooker, of jazz musicians like Wes Montgomery and Pat Metheny, of folkies and rockers like Dylan himself, and of an array of musicians from many tantalizing world-music traditions. With luck, John Mabry will write a book about those influences someday as well.

Still, tracking the influence of one artist on another can be a tricky business, as literary phenomenologists and New Critics will tell you, but Mabry has navigated it masterfully, due in no small part, I'm sure, to the fact that he himself opened his eyes and ears to both of those artists. Mabry is not just a scholar of intense perception, able to detect subtle cultural and theological connections, but a formidable fiction writer and musician in his own right. I can think of no living author whose published and recorded works so deeply partake of the legacies of Williams and Cockburn. Like Williams, Mabry has written books of poetry, theology, criticism, religious history and biography, but most especially fiction, true spiritual thrillers in the tradition of Williams and other great writers of fantasy and science fiction; and his music is imbued with the spirit of Bruce Cockburn and many other rock, punk, jazz, and folk artists.

Simply put, no writer is as qualified to write a book about the affinities between Charles Williams and Bruce Cockburn as John Mabry. He is a kindred spirit, a link in an enduring, provocative literary chain, a third interlocutor in Williams's and Cockburn's intense theological conversation, or, dare I say, almost like a belated Inkling.

The last track on Bruce Cockburn's 1976 album *In the Falling Dark* evokes a time when Jesus will return to lead his followers to a "festival of friends." I am thrilled by the possibility —the assurance, really—that Charles Williams, Bruce Cockburn, and John Mabry will have a chance to sit together and talk, to share ideas, and to listen. Perhaps Cockburn and Mabry might even play some of their songs for Williams. That's a performance I'd like to see. Of course, I would love nothing more—such is my prayer—than to sit as near as I can to that elysian convocation and just take it all in. But until then, I'll settle for rereading *Shadows of Ecstasy and Rumours of Glory.*

—Robert Hudson, Ada, Michigan, June 2025
roberthudsonbooks.com

INTRODUCTION

While listening to Bruce Cockburn's 1979 album *Dancing in the Dragon's Jaws* for the first time, I was surprised to see the following in the liner notes: "The content of several of these songs has been influenced in varying degrees by the writings of Charles Williams." My eyebrows shot up. For those unfamiliar with Williams, I'm sure this meant little. But for those of us who know his work, this single sentence contained vast implications and invited scrutiny of Cockburn's lyrics in a whole new light.

From that moment, I was curious about what connections there might be between Cockburn's lyrics and Williams' ideas. How profound was the influence? How obvious? What parallels might reasonably be made between them? This book attempts to answer that question.

JUST WHO ARE THESE OBSCURE GENTLEMEN?

I am aware that some readers may be 1) familiar with Williams but not Cockburn, or 2) familiar with Cockburn but not Williams, and that 3) some will not have heard of either of them. If you, dear reader, are any one of the above, this section is for you.

Charles Williams in the 1930s.

Charles Williams (1886–1945) was a British writer most famous for seven novels that are sometimes described as "occult thrillers," a characterization that hardly does justice to their deep mysticism and idiosyncratic yet sincere Christianity. He considered himself first and foremost a poet, his crowning achievement being an incomplete but substantial collection of poems which remythologize the Arthurian legend in line with Williams' peculiar and wonderful theology. In addition to these, his prolific output included theology, plays, and literary criticism. Sadly, more people know who he is by extension than know him by his formidable body of work. After J.R.R. Tolkien and C.S. Lewis, Williams is reckoned the third most important member of the Inklings—an informal literary circle in Oxford, England that met regularly for gregarious fellowship, the consumption of much alcohol, and the delight of reading and critiquing one another's writing. It was in this circle of friends that *The Lord of the Rings* and the Narnia stories were first heard by any other living souls besides their authors. Williams had a profound influence on C.S. Lewis (less so on Tolkien, but it is there) and continues to exert his influence on anyone who reads him today (including, as we shall see, Bruce Cockburn).

Bruce Cockburn (1945–; his last name is pronounced "CO-burn") is a Canadian singer-songwriter sometimes referred to as "the Canadian Bob Dylan" (a dubious sobriquet he shares with Leonard Cohen). But Cockburn doesn't need comparisons with anyone to bolster his reputation—in a career spanning more than fifty years he has produced thirty-seven albums, twenty-two of which have been certified gold or platinum. He has won thirteen Juno awards (Canada's equivalent to the Grammys). He was made a member of the Order of Canada and has been awarded six honorary doctorates, including one in divinity from Queen's University, Toronto. "I am a Christian songwriter," Cockburn admits. "I just don't fit the Christian music scene."[1] Indeed, Cockburn's art isn't "Christian music" in the sense of evangelism dressed up as pop. He is, instead, a musician of deep integrity, peppering his observations of ordinary life with mystical insights that prick our souls and make us go, "Ah, yes, I know just what that is like." He has spent his career in the secular music industry, famous in his native Canada but eternally just on the verge of stardom in the United States. Renowned for his unique and complex guitar playing, it is his lyrics which often take center stage—rapid-fire images at once commonplace and yet evocative of the transcendent, often confessional, deeply mystical, frequently confrontational, and possessed of an honesty so naked that it demands reflection.

Bruce Cockburn in concert in Eugene, Oregon on July 31, 2003. Photo by Daniel Keebler.

MYSTICAL ORIENTATIONS

On December 30, 1969, in the liminal interval between the opening of ritual space and the sealing of a sacrament, Bruce Cockburn experienced a mystical vision that would not have been out of place in one of the novels of Charles Williams. As Cockburn describes it,

> ...when I held [my fiancé] Kitty's hand to place her ring, I became aware of a presence standing there with us—invisible to the eye but as solid and obvious as any of the people in the room. I felt bathed in the figure's energy. I shivered and said to myself, "Well, I don't know who or what this is, but we're in a Christian church, so it's got to be Jesus." Who else would it be? He spoke no words, but the presence was real, male, and loving.[2]

This dramatic in-breaking of Divine life into ordinary reality affected the trajectory of Cockburn's life in a way that readers familiar with any of Williams' protagonists will recognize. It put him on "a narrow path to a life to come / that explodes into sight with the power of the sun."[3]

Cockburn's lyrics revealed a spiritual hunger and mystical orientation from the very beginning of his career, long before encountering Williams, tendencies that grew in intensity as his confidence as an artist increased through the 1970s. In 1976, the year before he was introduced to Williams, Cockburn wrote lyrics that foreshadowed the mystical kinship he was soon to discover:

Light pours from a million radiant lives,
off of kids and dogs and the hard-shelled husbands and wives.
All that glory shining around, and we're all caught taking a dive.
And all the beasts of the hills around shout, "Such a waste!
Don't you know that from the first to the last
we're all one in the gift of grace?"[4]

And in "Lord of the Starfields," from the same album, Cockburn utters a mystical prayer worthy of Meister Eckhart: "Oh love that fires the sun, keep me burning."[5]

Sometime around 1977, Ross and Kathy Sharwin of Edmonton, Alberta, must have had some glimmer of the affinity Cockburn would have with Williams, because they gave him a copy of one of the novels and urged him to read it. In his 2014 autobiography, Cockburn elaborates:

> As for C. S. Lewis, I read a lot of his books, and though I never completely accepted all of his conclusions, I appreciated his willingness and ability to reason, as a Christian apologist and Oxford professor: to study and philosophize around the Divine and to articulate his careful insights. His little literary group, the Inklings...produced volumes of inspiring, insightful, and even revolutionary writings—none more so than Williams, who was a terrible writer but had an astounding vision of how

> Divine/human interaction works... I steamed through all seven of his novels and a volume of very dense poetry in the period between recording *Further Adventures Of* and the album that followed, *Dancing in the Dragon's Jaws*.[6]

We might rightly take issue with his assessment of Williams as "a terrible writer," but any honest reader will know what he means. Williams can make for difficult reading, many of his characters lack dimensionality (especially in his early novels), and often climactic scenes suffer from an opacity that leaves readers shaking their heads and muttering, "What the hell just happened?"

These are common complaints. As a review of *Descent into Hell* in *The London Supplement* quipped, "Mr. Williams has a brilliant imagination which often passed behind the clouds."[7] Williams' friend Anne Ridler was clear-eyed about his powers, writing that "In Williams, the intellectual gifts were greater than the aesthetic."[8] Yet for all his shortcomings as a prose stylist, we keep returning to Williams (and some of us spend our lives studying him), because his vision is breathtaking. And in Cockburn's case, he found in Williams a kindred soul, whose depth of spiritual insight was similar to his own.

Williams' themes started showing up in Cockburn's songs almost immediately. While Cockburn says that he read the novels after recording *Further Adventures Of* (1978), I believe he must have read at least a couple (probably *War in Heaven* and *The Greater Trumps*) before that album was completed—as we shall see, there are striking ideas and images in common between those books and that album. Nevertheless, there was a dramatic increase of influence on his next album, *Dancing in the Dragon's Jaws* (1979), about which he says,

> The album was influenced partly by the fact that during the period that songs were being written I read all of the works of Charles Williams, who is an English writer with a particularly

> pronounced ability to describe spiritual things in very vivid terms. Most of his books are novels. They're sort of mystery novels almost, that deal with different elements of the occult, but bringing it around to a Christian point of view. And his own particular experience seems very strange. There's a sense of depth of being in those novels that is really both disturbing and thrilling at the same time. Anyway, that kind of pervaded the writing of the songs because the books were so much in my head at the time.[9]

AFFINITIES

When I posted pictures of Williams and Cockburn side by side in anticipation of this book on Facebook, one friend wondered if they shared the same optometrist. So, sure, for what it's worth, both men shared an affection for round miner's glasses (as did John Lennon). But there are many other points of connection between the two men—as well as obvious places their lives diverged.

Williams died on 15 May, 1945. Twelve days later, Bruce Cockburn was born. The two are therefore part of very different generational cultures, and the worlds they grew up in were very different places, both in terms of geography and the world events that shaped them. Yet similarities abound. Both men cultivated a love of poetry in their youth. Cockburn says of his poetic influences,

> "Initially I listened to people like Dylan and John Lennon, and that was a big source of motivation to get writing in the first place, but ever since I discovered T.S. Eliot in high school I think I've been wired to poetry. Eliot would be one...sort of as an original influence... But really, a lot of different people, again. Alan Ginsburg is one, William Burroughs, even though he's not a poet...the whole beat scene had a profound effect on me, actually...at a formative stage in my life... All those French Poets,

> Rimbaud and a guy named Blaise Cendrars was a fantastic influence."[10]

And of course, both men went on to become respected poets in their own right—just because Williams could not carry a tune in his hat let us not begrudge the fact that Cockburn sings his poetry. Of his own work, Cockburn said, "It always seemed to me that if you're going to bother putting words to music, you should aim as high as you can in terms of style and content, just as poets do. That has been the starting point for my efforts over the years."[11]

Also formative to both men was an interest in the occult. Charles Williams was involved with A.E. Waite's Golden Dawn offshoot, The Fellowship of the Rosy Cross (FRC) from 1917 through about 1927 or so, and maintained close friendships with Golden Dawn members. The hermetic and esoteric philosophies he acquired during his time with Waite and his Golden Dawn fellows were to have profound influence on his worldview, his art, and his spirituality long after he ceased participating in the FRC.

In part, it was this background that intrigued Cockburn. In his autobiography, he writes,

> "When a fan gave me a copy of *War in Heaven*, I discovered a Christian author whose background in the occult paralleled my own. Williams was able to spin stories that respected the more worthy of those disciplines by giving them a place in the Christian universe."[12]

Yet Cockburn's interest in the occult was not as intense. It was, he said, "a transitory flirtation. But after a couple of years, I sort of decided I'd had enough of that. I just didn't like what it did to people. It was kind of like cocaine for the spirit. It wasn't all worthless. It wasn't all negative. But it was very unhealthy spiritually, I think."[13] One can find hermetic ideas in Cockburn's early music, as in this song from 1970:

Seasons turning yet again,
the Mother's breast is full again.
As in heaven, so with men,
is now and ever shall be.[14]

An indisputably positive influence on both men, however, was their association with the Anglican churches of their respective countries. Cockburn did not grow up particularly religious, but his girlfriend and later wife, Kitty, was a Christian. Their discussions opened him to the possibility that there might be something to the whole "Jesus thing." He said, "Eventually I realized that I was in fact a Christian in every way except getting down on my knees and saying, identifying myself with Jesus as a person. And I did that. And then I was a Christian."[15] For many years after his conversion, Cockburn attended an Anglican Church, and its spirituality—including its sacramentality and mysticism—were vital to his spiritual formation.

Both men went on to become "outsider" voices in the Christian community. T.S. Eliot once wrote to Williams, "One of your most important functions in life is to instill sound doctrine into people (tinged sometimes with heresy, of course, but the *very best* heresy) without their knowing it."[16] Williams' "heresies," as well as his unrepentant involvement in the occult, presents a stumbling block to many Christian readers, especially those who come to Williams via the more orthodox-friendly writing of C.S. Lewis.

Cockburn is likewise given the side-eye by many Christians, especially those of an evangelical bent, for whom right belief is given greater value than right relationship or right action. In his autobiography, Cockburn relates a story of a visit from Glenn Kaiser, a popular evangelical Christian musician. Upon learning that Cockburn and his girlfriend were living together but not married, he promptly left in a huff and instructed those in the Christian commune he led to divest themselves of any and all of Cockburn's music.[17] Cockburn's songs often present as sex-positive, and not always in ways most Evangelicals would approve.

Likewise, his penchant for profanity—both in his lyrics and in conversation—trouble many conservative Christians. His political views are almost aggressively progressive, bolstered by time spent in war zones as a reporter for Oxfam and other international aid organizations over the years. And many Christians do not know what to do with the pervasive mysticism that color his songs—it is unlike anything else in Christian music, and its depth and implications make many uncomfortable.

Yet in contrast to the mysticism so present in the works of these two men, they are both products of a skeptical century. C.S. Lewis wrote,

> ...there lived in Williams a sceptic and even a pessimist. No man —and least of all the common run of antitheists—could have written a better attack on Christianity than he. He used to say that if he were rich enough to build a church he would dedicate it to St. Thomas Didymus Sceptic... He never forgot the infinite menaces of life, the unremitted possibility of torture, maiming, madness, bereavement, and (over all) economic insecurity which, as he said in *War in Heaven*, poisons our sorrows as well as modifying our joys."[18]

These "menaces" are prevalent in Cockburn's work as well, often residing side by side with images of great beauty and profundity:

Down on the plain of 10,000 smokestacks
trucks butt each other to establish dominance.
The newspaper next to me leans over and says, matter-of-factly,
"Sacred mountain towers above meadows"
—uh huh—and above us,
grim travellers in dawn skies.[19]

His "uh-huh" suggests that it is difficult to trust in a sacred dimension to the world when confronted with the ugliness of concrete and corruption and the tyranny of corporations and autocrats. In *Descent into Hell*, Williams describes Peter Stanhope as embodying a similar paradox:

> There was, in that latest poetry, no contention between the presences of life and of death; so little indeed that there had been a contention in the *Sunday Times* whether Stanhope were a pessimist or an optimist. He himself said, in reply to an interviewer's question, that he was an optimist and hated it.[20]

I have no doubt that Stanhope's response made Cockburn chuckle in recognition. Yet for both men, faith is not an innate quality that some people have and some people don't—it is a choice. In *Witchcraft*, Williams speaks of the "greatest of virtues—a deliberate belief in God."[21] Cockburn, too, seems to have chosen his Christianity, and depicts holding fast to it in the face of modern horrors as being a daily struggle.

Derailed and desperate,
how did I get here?
Hanging from this high wire
by the tatters of my faith.

Sometimes a wind comes out of nowhere
and knocks you sideways.
And look, see my tears,
they fill the whole night sky.[22]

But for all their sincerely held Christian faith (however idiosyncratic), they are both remarkably open to the salvific potential of other faith traditions. Taking a cue from the Islamic tradition of listing and adoring the Ninety-Nine Names of God (the Provider, the Just, the Knower, the Most Merciful, etc.), Williams rarely uses the words "God" or even "Jesus" in his novels, instead preferring to speak of the Omnipotence, the Unity, the Protection, the Resignation, the Infinity, or the simply personified Love —qualities that are not the proprietary domain of any one particular religion, always capitalized to indicate their reference to Divinity. One of his personal mottos was, "Under the Mercy," a valediction also employed on his gravestone.

Cockburn borrows the latter directly in his lyric for "Fascist Architecture":

I've been in trouble, but I'm ok.
Been through the wringer, but I'm ok.
Walls are falling, and I'm ok.
Under the Mercy, and I'm ok.[23]

In various places, Cockburn also refers to God as personified Love, Light, Mystery, and (most delightfully) Big Circumstance:

Big Circumstance comes looming
like a darkly roaring train.
Rushes like a sucking wound
across a winter plain,
recognizing neither polished shine
nor spot nor stain,
and wherever you are on the compass rose,
you'll never be again.[24]

In his novel *Many Dimensions*, Williams portrays Prince Ali and Hajji Ibrahim (both Muslims) as virtuous and sincere people of faith. As Glen Cavaliero notes, "This novel is concerned with Divine Unity, and in it Williams relates Christianity to other religions and traditions, demonstrating in the process its all-inclusiveness."[25] And while Williams cannot be lauded for his portrayal of Jewish people in his novels (he often portrays them as villains), Anne Ridler affirms that it is the Jewish book of mystical theology, *The Zohar*, that provided "the foundations of Williams' thought about the symbolism of the body, and of his lifelong attempt to develop an adequate theology of marriage."[26] Even if Williams' affirmation of other religions is mostly indirect, he is an equal opportunity offender when it comes to a more negative assessment: "Christianity," he writes, "like all religions, is, frequently, almost unmitigated boredom or even a slow misery, in which the command to rejoice always is the most difficult of all!"[27]

Meanwhile, Cockburn's interfaith openness is more explicit, frequently reporting on indigenous rituals that have moved him deeply, such as this account of Australian Aborigines singing the morning star into the sky:

Rising like lightspill from this sleeping town,
like the light in a lover's eyes.
Rising from the hearts of the sleepers all around,
all those dreamers trying to light the sky.

Burning, all night long.
Burning, at the gates of dawn.
Singing, near and far.
Singing, to raise the morning star.[28]

He is even more explicit and universal in writing new verses for the traditional Gospel song, "Twelve Gates to the City":

No matter which tribe you're born to there's a way in for you.
Come from any quarter—you can be a citizen too—
'cause there's twelve gates to the city, hallelu.[29]

At other times, Cockburn's interfaith openness takes the form of an apophatic, theological humility before an unfolding and incomprehensible Mystery:

Rhododendrons in bloom, sharp against spring snow,
remind me of another time in a Japanese temple:

there was a single orange blossom
at the wrong time of year—seemed like a sign.
When I looked again, it was gone.

Weavers' fingers flying on the loom,
patterns shift too fast to be discerned.
All these years of thinking, ended up like this,
in front of all this beauty, understanding nothing.[30]

While examples of Williams' influence on Cockburn are most densely concentrated in those albums produced between 1979 and 1981, Williams has a knack for changing people in a profound way. His ideas turned out to have a long tail, as detectable influences can be found in Cockburn's work from that time through to the present day. When asked by an interviewer what kind of influence Williams had on his music, Cockburn answered,

> Nothing really direct in that I took his ideas and used them on the album, but he has...an apparently unique view of life and his ability to describe sort of transcending his experiences in very vivid terms is really something... It's that aspect of Williams that really affected me.[31]

It is true that there is not much concept-to-concept mapping to be made between them. Both are poets and artists, and so we see in Cockburn's work allusions, hints, echoes—which is proper to one artist filtering the ideas and influences of another into new creative work. Williams himself rarely quoted Dante directly in his fiction, yet the poet's influence is pervasive. Still, Williams' influences are discernible and many.

I see three possibilities for each of these examples of influence:

1. Some connections can be attributed to direct, conscious influence in which Cockburn used—and

knew that he was using—ideas and images originating in Williams' work.

2. Some connections can be attributed to unconscious influence in which Cockburn, while steeped in Williams' ideas, synthesized them in ways that may have been opaque to him while writing them.
3. Some connections can be attributed to the similarities between the experiences of mystics in all times, places, and religious contexts.

Throughout this book, I do not opine as to which of the three may be true: I intend to simply point out those places in Cockburn's work where ideas and images proper to Williams are discernible. But by now I hope it is clear that Williams and Cockburn would have plenty to talk about over a pint of whiskey.

Let us now "listen in" on what some of those discussions might have included, drilling down into theological specifics both as stated in Williams' prose and reflected in Cockburn's lyrics. We will first tend to Williams' main ideas, which are so closely intertwined that they very nearly hang together as a systematic theology. After we have gotten a good grounding in Williams' thought (and Cockburn's interpretations of it) we will turn to important and recurring images found in both men's art.

---

1. "The Social Commentaries of Bruce Cockburn" by J.D. Considine, Sun Pop Music Critic, *Baltimore Sun*, 18 March 1988.
2. Cockburn, 115–116.
3. "Gavin's Woodpile," *FAO*.
4. "In the Falling Dark," *IFD*.
5. "Lord of the Starfields," *IFD*. *This line is also reminiscent of the 23rd canto of The Paradiso, wherein Christ is described as "the one sun which set all burning."*
6. Cockburn, 162.
7. Review of *DiH, The London Supplement*, 25 September, 1937. Quoted in the afterword to an as yet unpublished annotated edition of *DiH* prepared by Sarah Thompson.
8. Ridler, ix.

9. Bruce Cockburn interview with Phil Catalfo, "Music That Matters" Radio Programme, New Dimensions Radio, San Francisco, California,15 July 1986.
10. "Bruce Cockburn Interview, Old Waldorf, San Francisco," transcribed by Charles Wolff, from a tape of an interview with Bruce Cockburn on November 2, 1981 at The Old Waldorf, San Francisco, CA. Wolfe originally transcribed the poet's name as "Blaison Dryer," but this has been corrected by Dave Hedenstrom.
11. "A Conversation with Bruce Cockburn" by Andy Whitman, *Image,* Issue 84.
12. Cockburn, 162.
13. "A Rising Northern Star: A Canadian Bruce Cockburn Wins More U.S. Converts" by Brad Buchholz, *Dallas Morning News,* January 12, 1992.
14. "Spring Song," *BC.*
15. Interview with Cathleen Falsani at the Ann Arbor Book Festival, May, 2006.
16. T.S. Eliot to Charles Williams, 14 December 1940, Bodleian Ms. Res. c.137, f.2., quoted in Roukema, viii.
17. Cockburn, chap 13.
18. *Essays*, xii-xiii.
19. "Grim Travellers," *HU.*
20. *DiH,* 2.
21. *Witchcraft*, 309.
22. "The Whole Night Sky," *CoN.*
23. "Fascist Architecture," *HU.*
24. "Shipwrecked at the Stable Door," *BiC.*
25. Cavaliero, 70.
26. Ridler, xxv.
27. *Religion and Love in Dante*, 3.
28. "To Raise the Morning Star," *SF.*
29. "Twelve Gates to the City" *BoB.*
30. "Understanding Nothing," *BiC.*
31. Bruce Cockburn Interview, The Old Waldorf, San Francisco, CA, 2 November 1981.

PART I
THE IDEAS

When I set eyes on wonders,
I've got to wonder what they mean.

—Bruce Cockburn, "Outside a Broken Phone Booth
with Money in my Hand," *Further Adventures Of*, 1979.

1

THE INBREAKING OF THE REAL

C.S. Lewis summed up Williams' novels this way: "He is writing that sort of book in which we begin by saying, 'Let us *suppose* that this everyday world were at some one point invaded by the marvelous.'"[1] Indeed, each of Williams' novels follows a similar pattern:

1. We are introduced to a group of very ordinary people.
2. Into their midst some element of the Divine is cast.
3. We watch as they each react, spinning either toward salvation or damnation.

In Williams' first published novel *War in Heaven* (1930), that element is the Holy Grail; in *Many Dimensions* (1930), it is a magical stone from the crown of King Solomon; in *The Place of the Lion* (1931) the element is the fact that Platonic archetypes are taking form in the material world and terrorizing the English countryside; in *The Greater Trumps* (1932), the element is the ur-tarot deck, from which all other decks derive. In these four novels, there is a MacGuffin, a divine tchotchke that sets things in motion.

In Williams' other three novels, the pattern is the same, but the MacGuffin is more diffuse. In his earliest novel, *Shadows of Ecstasy*,[2] the element of the Divine is a person who may or may not be immortal; in *Descent into Hell* (1932), it is the Doctrine of Substituted Love that exerts its influence; and in Williams' last novel, *All Hallows' Eve* (1945), it is death itself that provides a heightened sense of the Real to which the characters react.

This may seem formulaic, but the stories play out in novel ways that have very different theological emphases, making each one compelling, enlightening, and satisfying in its own right. This "inbreaking" of the Divine Reality into mundane life is a common theme in mystical writing, and Williams is a master of depicting the sacredness of the ordinary; or as Blake described it, the ability

To see a world in a grain of sand
And a heaven in a wild flower,
Hold infinity in the palm of your hand
And eternity in an hour.[3]

Cockburn's lyrics are not usually narrative in form, but first-person autobiographical accounts, often confessional and concerned with interior states. He is no less concerned with the "inbreaking" of the Real, however.[4] In "After the Rain," he sings:

I'm blown like smoke and blind as wind,
except for when your love breaks in.
Maybe to those who love is given sight
to pierce the wall of seeming night
and know it pure beyond all imagining.[5]

More often, however, this inbreaking is aspirational, expressed as a desperate petition. This is a frequent theme for Cockburn, as seen in these brief examples:

I'm the rag in a bottle of gasoline,
longing to ignite.[6]

Pearl sky raining light like hail,
come on and pierce me.
Raining light like a vision of the holy grail,
come on and pierce me.[7]

Concrete vortex sucks down the wind.
It's howling like a blinded violin.
Oh tongues of fire, come and kiss my brow.
If I ever needed you, well I need you now.[8]

What does it take for what's locked up inside to be free?
Fold me into you, you know where I'm dying to be.
When my ship sets sail on that ocean of deep mystery,
I want to wait no more.[9]

Uptight lawyer on Damascus road
becomes a nexus where the light explodes.
Concentrated, overpowering sight,
two-way whirlpool churning up all time.
Infinity stoops to touch the human mind.
Oh, let me rest in the place of light.[10]

The most vivid example of the inbreaking of the Real, however, is one that Cockburn credits to Williams' *Place of the Lion*. In that novel, archetypes are on the prowl in rural England, absorbing into themselves the manifest "instances" of which they are the heavenly ideal—a giant butterfly represents Beauty, a massive lion symbolizes Strength, a horse indicates Speed, and an eagle, Truth. As one would expect, the sight of these gargantuan animals coursing over hill and dale like Godzilla causes chaos and panic for the people of the village of Smetham.

Of course, it all starts out quietly enough. In the opening scene, all the characters know is that there is a lion on the loose, probably escaped from a zoo or a traveling show. Grevel Lindop, in his 2022 introduction to *The Place of the Lion*, proposes that this setup was suggested by a popular 1927 book by J.W. Dunne, *An Experiment with Time*, in which the author recounts a dream in which a lion, escaped from a menagerie, was roaming through a cornfield. The author says he dreamed getting his rifle.[11]

For Cockburn, the lion also emerged in a dream—not once but twice—and represented for him not just strength in the abstract, but the nuclear strength that pervaded the Reagan-era Cold War environment. Cockburn says of that time,

> I have a relative who is involved in one of those kinds of government jobs where they can't say what they do. The part you can say involves monitoring other people's radio transmissions and breaking codes. At that time China and the Soviet Union were almost at war on their mutual border. And both of them had nuclear capabilities. I had dinner with this relative of mine and he said, "We could wake up tomorrow to a nuclear war." Coming from him, it was a serious statement. So, I woke up the next morning and it wasn't a nuclear war. [Laughs] It was a real nice day and there was all this good stuff going on and I had a dream that night...where there were lions at the door, but they weren't threatening, it was kind of a peaceful thing. And it reflected a previous dream that was a real nightmare where the lions were threatening.[12]

For Cockburn, his dreams, the nuclear fever of the time, and his recent immersion in Williams' *The Place of the Lion* resulted in one of his most popular songs, "Wondering Where the Lions Are":

Sun's up, uh huh, looks okay.
The world survives into another day,

and I'm thinking about eternity.
Some kind of ecstasy got a hold on me.

I had another dream about lions at the door.
They weren't half as frightening as they were before.
But I'm thinking about eternity.
Some kind of ecstasy got a hold on me.

Huge orange flying boat rises off a lake,
thousand-year-old petroglyphs doing a double take,
pointing a finger at eternity.
I'm sitting in the middle of this ecstasy.

And I'm wondering where the lions are...[13]

In this song, the Real breaks into ordinary life in no less dramatic fashion as in any of Williams' novels, and is undiminished by its having been a dream. The Real is the Real, and it shows up and does its work, leading the singer to "ecstasy," one of Williams' favorite words.

---

1. Lewis, C.S. (24 November 2007), https://www.youtube.com/watch?v=Z5w134gYz04
2. *SoE* was most likely written in 1926, but not published until 1933.
3. Blake, William. "Auguries of Innocence" (1803).
4. I am using "the Real" here, after the fashion of Evelyn Underhill, who used it as a euphemism for Ultimate Reality, the Divine, or God. See the preface to the first edition of *Mysticism: A Study in Nature and Development of Spiritual Consciousness* (London: Methuen & Co., Ltd, 1911).
5. "After the Rain," *DDJ*.
6. "Lily of the Midnight Sky," *WoW*.
7. "Civilization and Its Discontents," *TwN*.
8. "Incandescent Blue," *DDJ*.
9. "Wait No More," *YNSE*.
10. "The Light Goes On Forever," a 1981 rarity found on the reissue of *ICF*, 2002.
11. J.W. Dunne, *An Experiment With Time*, Chapter XII. For A.H.E. Lee's article on Dunne's book, see "Time and Mr Dunne," *The Speculative Mason*,

Vo. XXXI No 2, April 1939, pp. 43–50 and No 3: July 1939, 93–6. Suggested by Lindop, *PoL*, vii.

12. "Closer to the Light with Bruce Cockburn" by Paul Zollo, *SongTalk*, vol. 4, issue 2, 1994.
13. "Wondering Where the Lions Are," *DDJ*.

2
THE WAY OF AFFIRMATION

In *The Greater Trumps*, Williams presents us with a couple in love, Henry and Nancy. They are at a dinner party hosted by Nancy's father, Mr. Coningsby, who has just inherited an ancient deck of tarot cards. Henry is of Gypsy heritage, and takes it upon himself to relate a bit of the lore of the cards to Nancy and their friends. He mentions that the twenty-two cards that make up the Greater Trumps are "the meaning of all process and the measure of the everlasting dance." Nancy asks him to tell them more. He points to a card featuring two lovers dancing down a road. "Unless you go with the hermit," Henry adds.[1] Summed up in these two cards—the Lovers and the Hermit—are two great approaches to spirituality that can be found not just in Christianity, but in nearly every religion.

The Lovers represents the Way of the Affirmation of Images (or, more simply, the Way of Affirmation), also known as the *via positiva*, the Positive Way. About this way, C.S. Lewis explained "that every created thing is, in its degree, an image of God, and the ordinate and faithful appreciation of that thing a clue which, truly followed, will lead back to Him."[2] This Way is also known as cataphatic spirituality, from the Greek κατάφάναι, "by means of speaking." This is the way of icons, of art, of music, of reveling in the body and the world and all of the sensual and erotic experiences to be found therein. In their proper place, every created thing points back to its Creator, and can act as a mediator of transcendent truth. Williams summed this Way up in the phrase, "Thou art that," a translation of the Sanskrit phrase, "*Tat tvam asi,*" found in the Chandogya Upanishad.[3] Anything one can point to—the sun, a tree, one's spouse, all are reflections of the Divine. By experiencing the world, we experience something of God.

Conversely, the Hermit—retreating from the world—represents the Way of the Rejection of Images (the Way of Rejection, the Ascetic Way, *via negativa*, or the Negative Way), also known as apophatic spirituality (ἀπόφημι, "without speaking"). This Way holds that there is nothing you can say about God that can in any way actually be true, since all of our words, metaphors, symbols, and concepts fall short of describing God's infinity—so it is best to simply say nothing. As Meister Eckhart so memorably put it, "The most beautiful thing which a person can say about God would be for that person to remain silent from the wisdom of an inner wealth. So, be silent and quit flapping your gums about God."[4] Williams' shorthand for this was, "Neither is this Thou," adapted from the Sanskrit, "*Neti, neti,*"[5] "not this, not that."

While most traditions lean toward one of the two ways, both can usually be found. The tension has been admirably maintained in Christianity: the defeat of the iconoclasts ushered in a great tradition of art that continues to the present day, while the monastics and the apophatic mystics continue to remind us that every image falls short. As Gavin Ashenden notes, "They are not to be alternatives to each other, but complementary. They need each other as antidotes to their own excesses."[6] Williams explained,

> Our Lord the Spirit is reluctant to allow either of the two great Ways to flourish without some courtesy to the other... The one Way was to affirm all things orderly until the universe

> throbbed with vitality; the other to reject all things until there was nothing anywhere but He. The Way of Affirmation was to develop great art and romantic love and marriage and philosophy and social justice; the Way of Rejection was to break out continually in the profound mystical documents of the soul, the records of the great psychological masters of Christendom. All was involved in Christendom, and between them, as it were, hummed the web of the ecclesiastical hierarchy.[7]

Both Williams and Cockburn are acolytes of and evangelists for the Way of Affirmation. They share a full-throated embrace of earthy, bawdy, bodily life, holding forth its messiness and its glory in two hands. In Williams, living out this embodied spirituality was mostly aspirational, desiring it and affirming it while at the same time being constrained by the vestiges of Victorian morality that still held sway in early 20th-century Britain. For Cockburn, however, as a child of the 1960s—with its embrace of sex, drugs, and rock-n-roll—a more liberal attitude prevailed. But both men struggled against the push-and-pull of their ascetic and libertine tendencies, and examples of both Ways can be found in their work, sometimes within the same sentence. For example, few poets have summed up the *kenosis* of sexual intimacy quite as vividly as Cockburn:

When two lovers really love, there's nothing there
but this suddenly compact universe
of skin and breath and hair.[8]

There is not a whiff of the ascetic or the Puritan in this verse. Nor is there the affirmation that such intimacy is (must!) be happening within the biblical covenant of marriage, as one expects from most Christian music. Instead, Cockburn simply presents the naked, human, ecstatic facts, leaving the moralizing to those who care about such things.

1. *GT*, 16.
2. *Arthurian Torso*, 335.
3. Chandogya Upanishad, chapter 6.
4. *Eckhart*, 44.
5. Brihadaranyaka Upanishad, II iii 1–6.
6. Ashenden, 62.
7. *Descent of the Dove*, 31, 58.
8. "The Coldest Night of the Year," *MD*.

3
CO-INHERENCE

The fundamental fact of the universe, as Williams saw it, is that all things in heaven and earth are part of an undivided Whole—all things depend on each other, all things are members of one another, and all things interpenetrate one another. He called this "co-inherence."[1]

On the most material level, we can see this lived out in the fact that our lives are dependent on the labor of others, and their lives are dependent on ours—we need the mechanic to fix our car, the butcher to provide meat, the farmer to grow our carrots. The supermarket checker takes money—the product of our labor—in exchange for food. Even if we were to retreat to the country to live "off the grid," it is the animals of the forest who provide our meat and the trees that grow the apples—trees that breath what we exhale and are nourished by our waste. The mutual dependence is inescapable.

This is what C.S. Lewis called the "economic and political mode" of co-inherence, which "has to do with goods and services. Natural law obtains; man's duty and privilege is to accept freely his rightful place in a republican and yet hierarchical order of creation."[2] As Williams wrote, "We may or may not live *for* others, but whether we like it or not, we do live *from* others."[3]

But there are two other modes operative in Williams' theology as well. Next there is the "relational mode," in which people are part of one another and belong to one another—we see this manifest in something as sacred as a marriage, and as quotidian as a bowling league. This is the realm of family and friendship, membership in clubs and societies, and in spiritual communities such as churches, synagogues, sanghas, and 12-Step meetings. Our dependence upon one another in this mode is emotional as well as pragmatic; life is hard, and so, because we love one another, we help each other.

Williams writes, "Our natural life begins by being borne in another; our mothers have to carry us. This is not (so far as we know) by our own will. The Christian Church demands that we shall carry out that principle everywhere by our will—with our friends and with our neighbours, whether we like our neighbours or not."[4] Elsewhere in the same essay, he writes, "We have, first, to learn that others exist by ceasing to resent their existence. Until we have ceased to resent that existence, merely instinctively, we can hardly be said to admit it. But having admitted it, we have then to decide what we are to do about it; what our attitude is to be towards those other existences, what our relation with them."[5]

The third mode of co-inherence is mystical and cosmic, and is grounded firmly in Christian doctrine. Williams was reported to have said, "It is not good for God to be alone,"[6] and indeed orthodox Christian faith sees God as a trinity—a community—of persons. While the doctrine of the Trinity is incomprehensible to some, for Williams it revealed a profound truth—true not just about God, but about all things. The doctrine of *perichoresis* (περιχώρησις) asserts that while the Father, Son, and Holy Spirit are distinct persons, they nevertheless mutually indwell one another. The Father is in the Son as the Son is in the Father; the Son is in the Spirit as the Spirit is in the Son; and the Father is in the Spirit as the Spirit is in the Father. The three are separate but interdependent and interpenetrating entities. Together—and only together—do they make up the community we worship and call God.

Christian doctrine further holds that the act of baptism unites us with Jesus.[7] He is in us as we are in him, and because we are united to him, we are in union with everyone else united to him. As Williams explained,

> Certainly the great Christian doctrine applied first to the "household of faith." Our Lord promised to the members of His Church a particular and intense union with each other through Himself. He defined that union as being of the same nature as that which He had with His Father. The later definitions of the inspired Church went farther; they declared not merely that the Father and the Son existed co-equally, but that they existed co-inherently—that is, that the Son existed *in* the Father and that the Father existed *in* the Son. The exact meaning of the preposition there may be obscure. But no other word could satisfy the intellect of the Church. The same preposition was used to define our Lord's relations with His Church: "we in him and he in us." It was in that sense that the Church itself in-lived its children: "we are members one of another."[8]

Most gloriously yet, because we are united to Jesus, we are invited to participate in the life of the Trinity as we are assembled into the community that is the Son (the "Body of Christ"). Since the Son is in the Father and the Spirit, the Father and the Spirit are in us as well. Jesus says as much in his high priestly prayer in John's Gospel: "I ask...that they may all be one...as you, Father, are in me and I am in you, may they also be in us."[9] Cockburn sings his prayer: "*You be in me and I'll be in you, / together in eternity.*"[10] Likewise, the Creed of St. Athanasius asserts, "Who although he is God and Man; yet he is not two, but one Christ. One; not by conversion of the Godhead into flesh; but by assumption of the Manhood into God."[11] As theologian Scott McKnight writes, *perichoresis*

> ...establishes what really is. Genuine, final reality for humans is to participate in the reciprocal interiority of the Trinity in Christ through the Spirit, and to extend this interiority to others as an approximation of that perichoresis. Genuine reality then is relational; genuine atonement is reconciliation... Atonement finally concerns union with God and, simultaneously, communion with one another as its mirror among God's created beings.[12]

But there is a cosmic dimension to this indwelling as well. In the incarnation event—when God became human, born into the body that Mary would name Jesus—God united himself with matter, with dust, with the earth, and with the whole of the created order. The Epistle to the Ephesians puts it this way:

> [God] set forth in Christ, as a plan for the fullness of time, to gather up all things in him, things in heaven and things on earth... He who descended is the same one who ascended far above all the heavens, so that he might fill all things.[13]

Thus, it isn't only Christians who (through baptism) have been ushered into the divine life of the Trinity, but all created things by virtue the Incarnation which occasioned the union of all things with Christ. This divine life includes the blessed company of those who have passed from mortal life into life eternal.[14]

Thus, because all things are in union (in God, or "in Love" as Williams was fond of saying) all things depend on all others, all things interpenetrate, all things are in relation to one another and to the whole. It is for this reason that the occult correspondences work. As Henry explains in *The Greater Trumps*, "All things are held together by correspondence, image with image, movement with movement: without that there could be no relation and therefore no truth. It is our business—especially yours and mine—to take up the power of relation. Do you know what I mean?"[15]

In an interview, Cockburn mentions the concept almost in passing: "Love—with a big L—Love, which understands the inexplicable interconnectedness of everything."[16] Cockburn tries to explicate it, however, in the lyrics to "Call It the Sundance":

Everything you do, everything you say,
whether false or true, in some kind of way,
touches something.
Everything you take, everything you leave,
every move you make, pulls the fabric of the weave
of everything.[17]

The image of pulling on a thread and affecting the whole cloth is very similar to one of Williams' favorite images for the Whole, the "web of glory." As early as 1925, the image makes an appearance in a poem:

O Earth's body, what pain
Tightens the whole fine nervous web?[18]

It was an image he would return to again and again. He makes splendid use of it in "Taliessin at Lancelot's Mass":

Then the Byzantine ritual, the Epiclesis, began;
then their voices in Ours invoked the making of man;
petal on petal floated out of the blossom of the Host,
and all ways the Theotokos conceived by the Holy Ghost.

We exposed, We exalted the Unity; prismed shone
web, paths, points; as it was done
the antipodean zones were retrieved round a white
rushing deck,
and the Acts of the Emperor took zenith from Caucasia
to Carbonek.

...That which had been Taliessin rose in the rood;
in the house of Galahad over the altar he stood,

manacled by the web, in the web made free;
there was no capable song for the joy in me...[19]

This is a glorious vision of oneness—or "Unity" as Williams called it—similar in many ways to panentheistic Christianity, Whitehead's Process Theology, and the Vishishtadvaita (qualified non-dualism) Vedanta of Ramanuja. As one might expect of a vision so grand, one metaphor could never bear the weight of it. Williams was also fond of "pattern" to describe the Way of Heaven. "The Empire is the pattern; Logres the experiment," he writes in "Notes on the Arthurian Myth,"[20] equating "the Empire" with what Jesus called "the Kingdom" and "Logres" with the imperfect attempt to live that pattern out on a fallen planet. As he laments in "The Index of the Body," "however...the vision of a patterned universe is revealed to us, the revelation vanishes, and we are left to study it slowly, heavily, and painfully."[21]

Williams was also fond of the metaphor of the "diagram." In *The Figure of Beatrice*, he speaks of mystics generally as "all who, tranced to intellectual joy, retrieve the diagram of glory."[22] Writing elsewhere of Dante's work, he combines the two metaphors: "...the question here is whether this pattern...is a pattern to us; whether the diagram of romantic love which it presents, with every circumstance of tenderness and terror, is a diagram of value to us."[23] In a collect composed for a proposed religious order dedicated to the awareness and celebration of co-inherence, he wrote, "Blessed be He that He has made us members one of another and all members of Him... Blessed be He that He has quickened among men the unity, exchange and substitution of love which is the pattern of Himself... Blessed be He that He continually makes all things new."[24]

Perhaps Cockburn's favorite image, which recurs frequently in his work, is that of ripples flowing out across the surface of water when a pebble has been cast into it. He even called his 1977 live album, "Circles in the Stream." "You throw the stone in the water and the circles spread," he wrote. "You can't tell what they pass through or where they'll stop."[25]

He uses this image in his Christmas song, "Cry of a Tiny Babe," reflecting on the continuous but often unseen impact of the Incarnation:

Like a stone on the surface of a still river,
driving the ripples on forever,
redemption rips through the surface of time
in the cry of a tiny babe.[26]

Ripples, diagram, pattern, web—all are images of the Whole, the Unity, the great interconnection in which all things participate, and indeed, co-inhere.

---

1. Stephen Barber writes: "The term co-inherence, always spelled thus by Williams, he took from G. L Prestige's 1938 study, *God in Patristic Thought...* Fiddes grants that these ideas are pervasive in all Williams's work but points out that he did not actually start using the term until 1939, notably in *The Descent of the Dove.*" Barber, *Patterns*, 134.
2. *Arthurian Torso*, 141–43.
3. Quoted in Shideler, 11.
4. "The Way of Exchange," *Image of the City, 152–3.*
5. *Ibid*, 148.
6. Ridler, xlv. In a footnote, Ridler says, "This aphoristic misquotation from Genesis is one I heard from Williams's lips: I think he ascribed it to Belloc, but my memory may be at fault."
7. Evangelical Christians would point to the act of "asking Jesus into one's heart" as marking the moment of this union and see baptism merely as a public proclamation of it.
8. "The Way of Exchange," *Image of the City*, 149.
9. John 17:20–24
10. "Wondering Where the Lions Are," *DDJ.*
11. The recitation of this creed is one of the emotional high points of Williams' novel *The Greater Trumps.*
12. McKnight, 16–17.
13. Ephesians 3:9–10; 4:10.
14. In "The Redeemed City," Williams wrote, "The noble republicans of earth, the great humanitarian champions, are to be welcomed with respect and

admiration. The lack in their vision of union is that they cannot include the dead." *Image of the City*, 102.

15. *GT*, 47.
16. surefich.co.uk: *Culture: Bruce Cockburn*, article by Martin Wroe, September 4, 2003.
17. "Call it the Sundance," from the 2003 reissue of *SF*.
18. "Domesticity," *Windows of Night*, 22–25.
19. "Taliessin at Lancelot's Mass," in *Taliessin Through Logres*, 108–109.
20. "Notes on the Arthurian Myth," *Image of the City*, 178.
21. "Index of the Body," *Image of the City*, 86.
22. *The Figure of Beatrice*, 178.
23. "Religion and Love in Dante," Barber, *Celian*, 67.
24. Newman, 9.
25. From the *World Of Wonders* Tour Program, circa 1986.
26. "The Cry of a Tiny Babe," *NBBL*.

4

ROMANTIC THEOLOGY

On one of his early albums, Bruce Cockburn sang,

In the place my wonder comes from,
there I find you.
Your face shines in my sky.

In your heart where the world comes from,
there you will find me.
Your eyes dance in my mind.

Come with me,
we will sail on the wind.
We will sway among the yellow grass.
When you be beside me,
I am real.[1]

Written and recorded more than five years before Cockburn was introduced to Williams, it reveals an artist predisposed to connect deeply with Williams' theology—the seeds of the Affirmative Way, a sensuous and sacramental spirituality, were already present.

For Williams' part, the development of his theology of romantic love seems to have been born in ambivalence. As Gavin Ashenden notes, "As an artist he dealt in the language of the Via Affirmativa; by nature, he was more drawn to the Via Negativa."[2] A young man in 1908, he had met and fallen in love with Florence Conway, and began writing poems for and about her. The subject of these poems was "renunciation." Compassion for the young woman confronted with such mixed messages is not misplaced—Charles dithered over which of the two ways (affirmation or negation) he would choose, putting off marriage for nine years.

Having taken the plunge, however, Williams committed to the Way of Affirmation, becoming perhaps its greatest literary advocate. In Williams' writing, we see romantic theology developing in three broad, interconnecting streams: 1) courtly love; 2) human love leading us to divine Love; 3) life lived "in" Love, with Christ as the pattern for all human life and loving. We'll talk about the first two in this section, while the third will become clear in our discussion of "Exchange" below.

Regarding the first stream, Williams was deeply influenced by the tradition of courtly love he found in Arthurian legend, but even more so in Dante's *Divine Comedy*. Courtly love is a medieval tradition rooted in a deep sense of longing for an unattainable love—usually a married woman. The lover projects his idealized notions of love onto the beloved, and it is the energy of his unconsummated ardor that drives his chivalrous career. (It is easy to see how Williams was already living out that myth while stringing poor Florence along.) But courtly love found its full flower in Dante, when the poet fell in love with Beatrice so deeply and completely that his quest for her ultimately leads him to the splendor of heaven.

As for the second stream, Williams believed that love in any form participates in—and leads us to—Love, which is deity's true name. Alice Hadfield neatly describes his project in a single sentence: "In experiencing romantic love, we experience God: He has been in the experience from the beginning, and the more we learn about it, the more we learn also about Him."[3] She continues,

> [Williams] meant, I think, by "romance" what John Buchan once called "strangeness flowering from the commonplace," or, if you like, making the ordinary extraordinary. For sex, love, and marriage are commonplace and ordinary; they can also and at the same time be strange and extraordinary. Romance, he felt, does not stand by itself; it is an aspect of the multiform relationship of men, women, and God, the study of which is theology's business. Romantic theology is, therefore, the working out of ways in which an ordinary relationship between two people can become one that is extraordinary, one that grants us glimpses, visions of perfection.[4]

In this theology, we find a powerful antidote to the vestigial Manichaeism of Augustine's theological legacy. Augustine was deeply suspicious of the body, of sensuality, of passion—and Western theology has carried on in his wake. But Williams was convinced that "the body has not, in fact, as some pious people suggest, fallen a good deal farther than the soul."[5] In Williams' theology, romantic love—and all the delicious carnality that comes with it—is sacramental, in that it is "an outward and visible sign of an inward and invisible grace."[6] Friendship, infatuation, and sex are not ends in themselves, and we distort their goodness and turn them into idols if we treat them as such. But as shadows of ecstasy and rumours of glory, they point beyond themselves to the archetypal Love of which they are mere but dear manifestations. Williams believed that this was not only what *The Divine Comedy* is "about"—it is, he says, "what Love is 'about.' It is what Love is 'up to,' and the only question is whether lovers are 'up to' Love... Wherever the 'stupor' is, there is the beginning of the art."[7]

Cockburn suggests a sacramental connection between sex and

the action of Love in our lives in his song, "Lovers in a Dangerous Time":

These fragile bodies of touch and taste,
this vibrant skin—this hair like lace.
Spirits open to the thrust of grace.
Never a breath you can afford to waste,
when you're lovers in a dangerous time.[8]

As we have seen in Williams' theology, a pronounced "as above, so below" sensibility is always present. In Cockburn's work, there is often a great deal of ambiguity about whether he is speaking to a human lover or to divine Love. When asked about it in an interview, Cockburn said, "When I'm writing the song, I'm entirely aware of which it is. To me [some songs] are pretty carnal. But sometimes when you're expressing longing for a person, deeper things creep into it. It's fair enough if people want to read it the other way."[9] These "deeper things" are inescapable in both Williams' and Cockburn's art because when we truly assent to loving another person, this love takes on cosmic scope, for in loving and assenting to be loved we embrace co-inherence and interdependence, and we learn to progressively offer up our own comfort for the good of another, and then others. If "God is love," then we cannot touch the face of our lover without touching the face of God.

Cockburn captures the dance between intimacy and ultimacy beautifully in his 1984 song, "Making Contact":

Step outside, take a look at the stars,
catch a glimpse of the way things are.
Making contact...

Smell of sweet fresh oil on skin,
when you move on me like the tide coming in.
Making contact...

I hear the drumming of the surf and I have to dance,
stepping to the rhythm of circumstance.
Making contact...

I feel so huge—I feel so small.
I feel so good I want to swallow it all.
Making contact...
Swimming in an ocean of love...[10]

"Making Contact" is the sudden awareness of co-inherence, of identity with the One, which can come about through awe at nature's vastness or the intimate touch of lovers' skin. It can come about through the ecstasy of dance as well as the ecstasy of gnosis. Cockburn's song is a beautiful and joyous expression of the diverse ways that embodied human life connects to—and participates in—the Life of All. In a later song, Cockburn expresses the same sense of intimate cosmic connection, but this time with an aching poignancy that recalls St. Paul's longing for a time when the universe need groan no more:[11]

What does it take for the heart to explode into stars?
One day we'll wake to remember how lovely we are.
Lightning's a kiss that lands hot on the loins of the sky.
Something uncoils at the base of my spine and I cry.
I want to wait no more.[12]

BABY STEPS

In true Williamsian fashion, even a single step in the direction of intimacy can eventually lead to Love. In *The Greater Trumps*, Sybil wonders if perhaps her tentative step toward a person she finds repellent might be of use to Love:

> She was uneasily conscious that she sometimes lured her butcher in London into showing off his pomposity, his masterful attitude towards his employees, because it seemed to her so wonderful that he should be able to behave so. "My fault," Sybil sighed to herself, and offered herself once more as a means whereby Love could more completely love the butcher. Not, of course, that Love didn't completely love the butcher already, but through her perhaps...however, that argument was for the theologians.[13]

Sybil's conviction that Love loved the Butcher is reminiscent of Cockburn's, "If you love Love, then Love loves you, too."[14] But more to the point of taking "baby steps" toward love is Cockburn's song, "And We Dance," in which he gives us what may very well be one of the most poetic descriptions of a hand job in all of popular music:

Down there in the realm of power
somebody's manicured hands
plays the ace of influence
against the jack of demands.

But in the next few lines the tawdriness of a not-too-well-hidden sex act at a party is redeemed:

I reach for the deck,
draw the seven of hearts.
It doesn't mean the world
but it's a better place to start.

The symbolism is obvious, of course, and in this verse Cockburn is making two assertions: that even casual sex can point us to Divine love, but that divine Love is clearly the superior form—both points on which I believe Williams would concur. In one scene after another in Williams' novels, the limited, selfish love of one character for another (for example, Lester's self-centered affection for Richard in *All Hallows' Eve*) is enough to give divine Love a foothold to do its redemptive work. In Martin Luther's theology, we are born with self-serving love, which is enough to get us started. The work of God in us is the transformation of our self-serving love into self-giving love, which is what God *is*. This is a peculiarly Protestant form of theosis,[15] wherein the Spirit makes use of our petty attempts at love (complete with all their ulterior motives) to begin a process, the end of which is to transform us into divine Love itself. In Cockburn's lyric, as in Williams' novels, the Spirit says of our meagre attempts to love, "Very well, then—this is an opening. Let us start here."

FEET OF CLAY

For all his exalted praise of romantic love, however, Williams is very aware indeed of how far short of perfect love we fall—himself included. In *Outlines of Romantic Theology*, he warns against an overly rosy view of the beloved:

> ...in love it is most certain that the lovers are manifest to each other's eyes in their original perfection; but this is not the same thing as the rather silly convention of romance that only a pretended criticism of the beloved should be allowed a place. The romantic mind must, if it is to be justified, work within the bounds of realism; as indeed love itself does, for of all proverbs that which declares that "Love is blind" is surely the most foolish. Love can only see the next world by virtue of that eyesight which sees and is not afraid to see the flaws in this; all other vision is blindness, all other faith superstition.[16]

Of Beatrice and Dante, Williams writes, "Her, or his, humanity is an extremely maculate humanity, and all the worship under heaven ought not to prevent her lover from knowing (with reasonable accuracy and unreasonable love) when she is lazy, lewd, or malicious. She has a double nature, and he can have double sight."[17]

Gender assignations aside, we might detect a bit of projection here, as "maculate" as Williams' own life was. In fact, it is impossible, with all that has been revealed about Williams' inner life, to paint a hagiographic picture of him. He was a deeply flawed man.

The worst of it was unfortunately all-too-mundane: he betrayed his wife Florence/Michel by entering into a years-long emotional affair with a co-worker, Phyllis Jones. While most Williams scholars agree that the relationship was never physically consummated, Williams neglected his wife's own needs for emotional intimacy and fixated on Jones as his own personal Beatrice, employing his fixation on her for the purposes of his own spiritual and creative fecundity, as odd as that sounds.

After the affair with Jones ended, he turned his attentions to a series of starry-eyed disciples, taking advantage of their infatuation with him to lure them into magickal workings punctuated by mild sadism. This involved sessions in which he dominated the women and inflicted physical pain on them for the sole purpose of raising sexual energy within himself, which he then redirected in service of his creativity. To be clear, he never had sexual relations with any of these women, and what they did with him, they did willingly. But there is no question that he used his charisma, celebrity, and authority (such as they were) to manipulate, objectify, and exploit women who looked up to him. The women themselves were deeply conflicted about these encounters and their ongoing relationship with their "guru."[18]

In addition to this, Williams was a neglectful father, ill-suited to parenthood temperamentally, and impatient with a child whose intellect could not match his own—and precious few could. Inheriting Charles' nervous physicality, his son Michael was prone to bouts of mental illness (especially depression), his distress amplified by the tension between his parents due to his father's emotional affairs. When Michael was still an infant, Charles wrote to a friend, saying:

> I cannot think of myself as a father; just occasionally, when I am playing with the Infant, I see far off, as in an illustration of 1850 in the *Sunday at Home*, a dreadful distortion of myself. It's the revolt, I think, of the contemporary imagination against its predecessor. The fatherhood of the fathers is visited upon their children and our teeth are set on edge. We can't, we daren't, be as consciously paternal... Anyhow, the child is bound to be unhappy.[19]

Williams did not want his secrets to be known, and would probably be horrified that scholarship has not turned a blind eye to his darker proclivities. But that does not mean that he was not self-aware. In his play, "The House of the Octopus," he writes,

> Every pious man—and of course, woman—
> has one, just one—surface where religion and he
> are so delicately mixed in his soul as to be
> indistinguishable; he is never quite sure—
> and does not (believe me!) ever want to be sure—
> whether his religion or he is being soothed
> into a lascivious spiritual delight.
> All of them, Prefect, are at bottom religious lechers,
> fornicating with their fancies.[20]

In his novel, *Descent into Hell,* Williams splits his own personality into two characters, Peter Stanhope and Lawrence Wentworth. (This is perhaps not surprising in a novel replete with doppelgängers.) Stanhope represents his Apollonian nature—the wise, kindly, and respected poet—while Wentworth represents his Dionysian side, full of professional jealousy, resentment, and pettiness. Wentworth stalks Adela Hunt, a woman he is in love with. The demon Lilith (masquerading as a suburban society crone named Lily Sammile) gifts him a double of Adela (another doppelgänger, and probably a succubus) whom he can possess, control, and sexually exploit for his own satisfaction. In a letter to

Anne Bradby, Williams admits, "There is—I sometimes think—the smallest flicker of Mr. Wentworth about me." As Charles Williams biographer Grevel Lindop put it, "This is an understatement."[21]

Although Cockburn has been accused of nothing so salacious, he has been quite open and confessional about his failings as a lover, husband, and father. He admitted to having his own "Beatrice," a married woman he was infatuated with who served as muse for his 1994 album, *Dart to the Heart*. In a song from that album, he sings,

Stars look down and laugh at me—
I ought to take a bow.
Don't have to tell them life's hard sometimes—
there's one falling now.
Nobody's here beside me
I can talk about it to—
all the ways I want you.[22]

In an interview, Cockburn reflected on the complexity of his own brush with "courtly love" and that particular aspect of Romantic Theology:

> Man, being in love with somebody I wasn't supposed to be in love with and reflecting on what that meant, ya know? The love, the feeling of love was totally real and seemed kind of God-given, but the object of that particular feeling was married to somebody else and there was nothing I could do about it. [Laughs.] So, there's a kind of ironic sense of God laughing and love being a significant part of that laughter.[23]

Most poignant, though, is his heartbreak over his divorce with his wife Kitty in 1980. It is clear from his songs that the breakup was not of his choosing. In a song on "Humans" he pleads with his wife,

What about the bond?
What about the mystical unity?
What about the bond,
sealed in the loving presence of the Father?[24]

On another song from that same album, however, he takes full responsibility for his part in the damage done to the marriage:

Fascist architecture of my own design.
Too long been keeping my love confined.
You tore me out of myself alive.

Those fingers drawing out blood like sweat,
while the magnificent façades crumble and burn.
The billion facets of brilliant love,
the billion facets of freedom turning in the light...

Gonna tell my old lady,
gonna tell my little girl,
there isn't anything in the world
that can lock up my love again.[25]

The song conveys a heart-rending epiphany, however too little and too late. There is an echo of Pink Floyd's "tear down the wall" in the destruction of the "magnificent façades"—cutting himself off from others, especially those he loves most, is not serving him. They must come down. In an interview, Cockburn commented,

> The image "fascist architecture" came from Italy. It was stuff that was built during Mussolini's period that was a particular style where the buildings are really larger than life and what is supposed to celebrate the greatness of humanity actually dwarfs humanity. And it makes you feel tiny and helpless next to it. And everybody hates this stuff. It seemed to me a suitable image for the things in ourselves, the structures we build that are built

> on false expectations or pretenses. The things we pretend to ourselves. And then when some catastrophe comes your way, like a marriage breaking up or some other thing, those things crack and you get glimpses through them, the light comes through them. It's not a comfortable thing.[26]

In a later interview, he said, "At the time I wrote it, my then marriage was in its final stages. So, there is that personal side; but the main point was just the idea of just being broken open by an intervention, I guess."[27] But whence came that intervention? When he sings, "You tore me out of myself alive?" who does the "you" in that line refer to—God? Jesus? his wife Kitty? an unnamed person who confronted him, Nathan-like, with his own sin? He doesn't say, but since this is his "peak Williams" period, I think it fair to ask if the "you" might be Williams.

Williams has certainly been the catalyst for repentance before. After reading *The Place of the Lion*, C.S. Lewis was moved to write a fan letter to Williams that occasioned their eventual meeting, in which he wrote, "I was in danger of becoming Damaris; but you have saved me."[28] In a letter to a friend, Lewis confides more:

> The reading of it has been a good preparation for Lent as far as I am concerned: for it shows me (through the heroine) the special sin of the abuse of intellect to which all my profession are liable, more clearly than I ever saw it before. I have learned more than I ever knew yet about humility. In fact it has been a big experience.[29]

Whoever it is that "tore" him out of himself alive, Cockburn has been very open about the fact that he underwent a significant transformation at this time. In an interview, he said,

> The tone of the albums really changes with *Humans*, which also coincides with my divorce, and the end of a decade and a point

> in my life that was partly triggered by the divorce and partly not, where I spent a lot of time looking at how my inner being related to the big picture, the cosmic picture, and it was time to include other people in that search for an understanding of relationship. To put it in simple terms: as a Christian, if you're gonna love your fellow mankind you gotta know who they are; you can't love them in the abstract. So it was time to kind of be among humans.[30]

It cannot be a coincidence that a statement so shot through with Williams' ideas comes shortly after Cockburn has immersed himself in his novels. His introduction to Williams' writings coupled with the dissolution of his marriage led to an uncurling of "the worm of the soul" and a turning toward an active and conscious co-inherence with God, nature, and other people. He has learned some hard truths about himself and the world:

Everybody's seen the things they've seen.
We all have to live with what we've been.
When they say charity begins at home
they're not just talking about a toilet and a telephone.[31]

Williams and Cockburn are flawed, messy, complicated people —just like the rest of us. Perhaps this is part of the reason they move us so. It is in their brokenness, their humanness, that we see ourselves most powerfully, poignantly, and clearly. Like all of us, their love is imperfect. And like all of us, it is enough for Love to work with.

---

1. "Love Song," *HWWS*.
2. Ashenden, 57.
3. Hadfield, xi.
4. Hadfield, viii.
5. "Sensuality and Substance," from *The Image of the City,* 68.
6. Ironically, a quote from Augustine, from "On the Instruction of the Uninstructed."

7. *The Figure of Beatrice,* 232.
8. "Lovers in a Dangerous Time," *SF.*
9. Boehm.
10. "Making Contact," *SF.*
11. Romans 8:22
12. "Wait No More," *YNSE.*
13. *GT,* 152.
14. "Love Loves You, Too," *D2H.*
15. Peura, 78.
16. *Outlines of Romantic Theology,* 12.
17. *He Came Down from Heaven,* 73.
18. See *Letters to Lalage: The Letters of Charles Williams to Lois Lang-Sims* (Kent, OH: Kent State University Press, 1989) and compare to the hagiographic portrayal of Williams presented by other female disciples with whom he also had emotional affairs, such as Alice Mary Hadfield and Anne Ridler.
19. Lindop, *3rd Inkling,* 120.
20. "House of the Octopus," *Collected Plays by Charles Williams,* 276–277.
21. Charles Williams to Anne Bradby, 30 Aug 1934, Bodleian ARP, quoted in Lindop, Grevel. *Charles Williams: The Third Inkling,* 277.
22. "All the Ways I Want You," *D2H.* See also, "Listen for the Laugh" from that same album.
23. From Sedge Thompson's interview on *West Coast Live,* 29 June 2002, at the Kate Wolf Memorial Music Festival in Laytonville, California.
24. "What About the Bond?" *HU.*
25. "Fascist Architecture," *HU.*
26. "Closer to the Light with Bruce Cockburn" by Paul Zollo, *SongTalk,* vol.4, issue 2, 1994.
27. From Canoe Online Chat with Bruce Cockburn, 15 January 2002.
28. Lindop, *PoL,* v. Damaris Tigh, a primary character in *PoL,* displays an appalling intellectual arrogance.
29. C.S. Lewis, 1936 Letter to Arthur Greeves, quoted in Carpenter, 99.
30. From Bruce Cockburn Interview, *Guitarist Magazine,* November, 1999, by Steve Lawson.
31. "Justice," *ICF.*

5

EXCHANGE & SUBSTITUTED LOVE

In *Descent into Hell*, a famous poet named Peter Stanhope counsels an anxious young woman named Pauline Anstruther, who is so afraid of meeting her doppelgänger that she fears for her mental health:

> "It comes from a long way off, and it comes up towards me, and I'm terrified—terrified—one day it'll come on and meet me. It hasn't so far; it's turned away or disappeared. But it won't always; it'll come right up to me—and then I shall go mad or die."
>
> "Why?" he asked quickly, and she answered at once, "Because I'm afraid. Dreadfully afraid."
>
> "But," he said, "that I don't quite understand. You have friends; haven't you asked one of them to carry your fear?"
>
> "Carry my fear!" she said... "How can anyone else carry my fear? Can anyone else see it and have to meet it?"

Stanhope offers to bear her fear himself, and explains with patience and compassion:

"We all know what fear and trouble are. Very well—when you leave here you'll think of yourself that I've taken this particular trouble over instead of you. You'd do as much for me if I needed it, or for any one. And I will give myself to it. I'll think of what comes to you, and imagine it, and know it, and be afraid of it. And then, you see, you won't... It's so easy...easy for both of us. It needs only the act. For what can be simpler than for you to think to yourself that since I am there to be troubled instead of you, therefore you needn't be troubled? And what can be easier than for me to carry a little while a burden that isn't mine?"

..."But that means—" she began, and stopped.

"I know," Stanhope said. "It means listening sympathetically, and thinking unselfishly, and being anxious about, and so on. Well, I don't say a word against all that; no doubt it helps. But I think when Christ or St. Paul, or whoever said *bear*, or whatever he Aramaically said instead of *bear*, he meant something much more like carrying a parcel instead of someone else. To bear a burden is precisely to carry it instead of. If you're still carrying yours, I'm not carrying it for you—however sympathetic I may be. And anyhow there's no need to introduce Christ, unless you wish. It's a fact of experience. If you give a weight to me, you can't be carrying it yourself; all I'm asking you to do is to notice that blazing truth. It doesn't sound very difficult."

"And if I could," she said. "If I could do—whatever it is you mean, would I? Would I push my burden on to anybody else?"

"Not if you insist on making a universe for yourself," he answered. "If you want to disobey and refuse the laws that are common to us all, if you want to live in pride and division and anger, you can. But if you will be part of the rest[1] of us, and live and laugh and be ashamed with us, then you must be content to be helped. You must give your burden up to someone else, and you must carry someone else's burden. I haven't made the universe and it isn't my fault. But I'm sure that this is a law of the universe, and not to give up your parcel is as much to rebel as

> not to carry another's. You'll find it quite easy if you let yourself do it."[2]

Pauline finally agrees to the odd proposition, and to her great surprise, as she is out walking, she notices with a start that she is enjoying herself.

> She wouldn't worry; no, because she couldn't worry. That was the mere truth—she couldn't worry. She was, then and there, whatever happened later, entirely free. She was, then and there incapable of distress. The world was beautiful about her, and she walked in it, enjoying. He had been quite right; he had simply picked up her parcel. God knew how he had done it, but he had. A thing had, everywhere and all at once, happened.[3]

This seems like fantasy, like magic. It *is* magic, of course, but (to paraphrase T.S. Eliot) it is the very best *sort* of magic, and Williams was dead serious about its efficacy in the real world. He grounded his thinking in Paul's epistle to the Galatians:

> "Bear ye one another's burdens, and so fulfil the law of Christ."[4] ...In exterior things it is recognized as valid—at least until we become bored; the fiftieth rather than the first visit to the sick is distasteful. Interiorly, it is less frequently supposed to be possible, and even exteriorly it has a wider range than is, perhaps, allowed. Saint Paul's injunction is to such acts as "fulfil the law of Christ," that is, to acts of substitution. To take over the grief or the fear or the anxiety of another is precisely that; and precisely that is less practised than praised... It is supposed to be for 'nuns, confessors, saints, not us': so much the worse for us. We are supposed to be content to "cast our burdens on the Lord." The Lord indicated that the best way to do so was to hand these over to someone else to cast, or even to cast them on him in someone else. There will still be work enough for the self, carrying the burdens of others, and

> becoming the point at which those burdens are taken over by the Divine Thing which is the kingdom: "as he is, even so are we in this world."[5]

He called this practice "exchange," and it is the logical outgrowth of his doctrine of co-inherence. If we are all connected, if our lives and the lives of others are physically, mentally, and spiritually woven together into an inseparable Unity, then there is no act that does not bear upon the lives of everyone else. To live in Love is to cooperate gladly with this Unity, rather than resenting or resisting it. We do that by assenting to our Union, and participating in it joyfully by carrying the burdens of others. Exchange is what co-inherence looks like in action. Co-inherence and Exchange are the noun and verb forms, respectively, of the same whole and interpenetrating Reality.

Williams expresses this beautifully and poetically in *Taliessin Through Logres*:

> ...that the everlasting house the soul discovers
> is always another's; we must lose our own ends;
> we must always live in the habitation of our lovers,
> my friend's shelter for me, mine for him.[6]

This practice is not unique to Williams, of course; it has a long (if often hidden) history in the Christian church. There is a story in the Desert Fathers in which it makes an early appearance:

> A brother had committed a grievous sin. He went to Abba Lot, and was very nervous, unable to sit. Abba Lot said, "What is the matter, brother?" He said, "I have committed a great fault and cannot acknowledge it to the priests." The old man said, "Confess it to me, and I will carry it." The brother said, "I made sacrifices at the pagan temple and bought time with the sacred prostitutes there as well." The old man rocked back and forth for a while. "This is not so bad," he said. "Don't be too hard on

> yourself. Go back to your cave, fast for a couple of days, and I will carry the blame for half of your transgression."[7]

Williams used another term to describe Exchange in such situations: "Substituted Love," by which he means the practice of substituting oneself for another—the exchange of one's own comfort to relieve the pain of another, the exchange of one's own innocence to relieve the sin of another, and so on. Williams looks to the life of Jesus, and most especially to the crucifixion, as the pattern or archetypical expression of this practice:

> We are to love each other as he loved us, laying down our lives as he did, that this love may be perfected. We are to love each other, that is, by acts of substitution. We are to be substituted and to bear substitution. All life is to be vicarious—at least, all life in the kingdom of heaven is to be vicarious... He would not only endure; he would renew; that is, accepting their act he would set up new relations with them on the basis of that act. In their victimization, and therefore in his, he proposed to effect an escape from that victimization. They had refused the co-inherence of the original creation, and had become (literally) incoherent in their suffering. He proposed to make those sufferings themselves co-inherent in him, and therefore to reintroduce them into the principle which was he. The Incarnation was to be a Redemption as well.[8]

Williams encouraged people he knew to practice Exchange for their friends and loved ones. He even formed a religious order, the Companions of the Co-Inherence, to study and employ Exchange as a spiritual discipline. In *He Came Down from Heaven*, he explains the particulars:

> There is, of course, a technique. If A is to carry B's burden he must be willing to do it to the full, even though he may not be asked to do it to the full. It is easy to sentimentalize, but the Day

> of Judgement exhibits our responsibilities in each case: 'at the hand of every man's brother will I require...' Messias may, now, carry the burden if we ourselves deliberately neglect or forget the agreement... It is therefore necessary (a) not to take burdens too recklessly; (b) to consider exactly how far any burden, accepted to the full, is likely to conflict with other duties. There is always a necessity for intelligence.[9]

Cockburn gives a nod to the practice of Exchange in his song, "Love Loves You, Too":

Some take the burden of another's pain.
Some spend forever for a moment's gain.
Everybody's got to find their own way through,
but if you love love, then love loves you too.[10]

While brief, the opening couplet of that verse contains everything that needs to be said about co-inherence, exchange and the choice before each and every soul to move toward salvation or damnation. A few years later, Cockburn would write the following chorus:

Wave on wave of life,
like the great wide ocean's roll.
Haunting hands of memory
pluck silver strands of soul.
The damage and the dying done,
the clarity of light,
gentle bows and glasses raised
to the charity of night.[11]

At first glance, the chorus seems to have little to do with Exchange, but Cockburn isn't talking about it in the abstract. His is almost always a first-person account. In an interview, he explained that it is the memories contained in the song itself that he finds burdensome, and that allowing others to hear them means he no longer has to carry them alone. He said, in language clearly patterned on Williams' ideas,

> What's the point of exposing these memories? Well, it's a way to help carry the baggage, you know? I mean from a selfish point of view, it's a way to get it off my chest and put it out there, hand it to someone else. And, from an unselfish point of view...it offers anybody who's got baggage of their own to carry—and we all do—a way of saying: Okay, I'm not the only one who has to carry this stuff. And that to me is what the whole "charity" thing—that's what I mean by the "charity of night" in a way... "The haunting hands of memory pluck silver strands of soul" is about carrying that baggage. It's about, it's these memories, just keep plucking at you, you know, playing notes. I mean, they're playing, they can play aggressive, savage notes or they can play beautiful notes.[12]

Although Cockburn has never mentioned reading Williams' theological writings, his experience is consonant with what Williams wrote in "The Redeemed City":

> ...an example of the truth that the vicarious and exchanged life which the Divine Spirit commands and communicates is not less but more inexorable than the individual and single, and that that also has its hierarchy and order of behaviour. In that life, as it moves in this life, the two shall be one; and the power which either draws on shall be double. This power may be for others besides them, but between them the opportunities of exchange are all to be thrown open. In this degree each may say, when the great experiment is done: "Myself I could not save; another I saved and another saved me."[13]

Cockburn is keenly aware of this vicarious quality of exchange, and its reciprocal demands prick his curiosity, even as he does not hesitate to take advantage of the help given to him. In "The Strong One," he sings,

When I was a torn jacket
hanging on the barbed wire
you cut me free
and sewed me up
and here I am.

Isn't it hard
to be the one whose phone rings all day every day?
Isn't it hard
to be the strong one?

Mouths move without vision—
without regard for consequences.
Eyes fill with memories
poisoned by intimate knowledge of the failure to love.
Sometimes, sometimes, doesn't the light seem to move so far away?
You help your sisters, you help your old lovers,
you help me, but who do you cry to?[14]

In the song, Cockburn isn't saying that the person he is singing to doesn't have someone to cry to, simply that he doesn't know who that person is. This is the mystery of the great web of Exchange. We trust that it's there, but we can't see it as it radiates out into the world. In this, it is a bit like the Communion of Saints—present, trustworthy, and invisible.

But the web of exchange tugs at us as well. Just as we have received, so it requires us to give. To refuse the giving would be to refuse the web itself, just as the refusal to be helped would be "to disobey and refuse the laws that are common to us all," as Stanhope told Pauline. In a later scene from *Descent into Hell*, Pauline finds herself cornered by Lily Sammile (aka Lilith). Lily's obsequiousness is suspicious, and when she tempts Pauline, her ruse is discovered:

> "Give me your hand," [Lily] said, "then come and dream, till you discover, so soon, the ripeness of your dreams." She paused, and added, "You'll never have to do anything for others any more."
>
> It was the last touch, and false, false because of the habit of her past and because of Stanhope's promise. The fountain of beauty had sprung upward in a last thrust; it broke against the arched roof of his world, and the shock stung her into coldness. Never have to do anything—and she had been promising herself that she would carry someone's parcel as hers had been carried, that she would be what he said she could. Like it or not, it had been an oath; rash or wise it stood...
>
> "An oath, an oath... Shall I lay perjury upon my soul?" The wind, rising as if to a storm, screamed "perjury" through the sky that held the Hill and all; false, false! she perjured in that last false gleam... Perjury, on her soul and in her blood, if now she slipped to buy sweets with money that was not hers; never, till it was hers in all love and princely good, by gift and gift and gift beyond excelling gift, in no secrecy of greed but all glory of public exchange, law of the universe and herself a child of the universe.[15]

The mood of this scene is dangerous—Pauline has dodged a bullet, and we feel the wind of the near-miss. In Cockburn's song, "The Gift" however, while the mood is jaunty and joyful, the message and the metaphor are the same:

In this cold commodity culture,
where you lay your money down,
it's hard to even notice
that all this earth is hallowed ground—

harder still to feel it,
basic as a breath.
Love is stronger than darkness.
Love is stronger than death.

The Gift
keeps moving—
never know
where it's going to land.
You must stand
back and let it
keep on changing hands.

Hackles rise in anger.
Heat waves rise in sex.
The Gift moves on regardless,
tying this world to the next.[16]

The "hands" image in this song has a precursor in Williams' novels. In *The Greater Trumps*, the primary symbol of Exchange is hands. Hands are mentioned 351 times in *The Greater Trumps*. By comparison, they are only mentioned 112 times in *Descent into Hell*. One scene in *The Greater Trumps*, which surely stands as one of Williams' most lysergically opaque, goes like this:

> Aaron was watching with growing horror the steady approach of the mist... The cloud was taking on form—he could not at first distinguish what the form was, and then at one point he suddenly realized he was looking at a moving hand, blocked out of the golden mist, working at something. It was the size of an ordinary man's hand, and then, while he looked, he missed it somehow, as a stain on a wall will be one minute a cat's head and the next but an irregular mark. But as he lifted his eyes he saw another—more like a slender woman's hand—from the wrist grasping upward at...at yet another hand that reached downward

> to it; and then those joining fingers had twisted together and became yet a third that moved up and down as if hammering, and as it moved was covered and hidden by the back of a fourth. His gaze swept the gathering cloud; everywhere it was made up of hands, whose shape was formed by it, and yet it was not the mist that formed them, for they were the mist. Everywhere those restless hands billowed forward; of all sizes, in all manner of movement, clasping, holding, striking, fighting, smoothing, climbing, thrusting out, drawing back, joining and disjoining, heaving upward, dragging down, appearing and disappearing, a curtain of activity falling over other activity, hands, and everywhere hands. Here and there the golden shimmer dulled into tints of ordinary flesh, then that was lost again, and the aureate splendour everywhere shone. The hands were working in the stuff, yet the stuff which they wrought was also hands, so that their purpose was foiled and thwarted and the workers became a part of that which was worked upon. Over and below and about the table the swelling and sinking curtain of mystery swept—if it were not rather through it, for it did not seem to divide or separate the movement, and the cloud seemed to break from it on the side nearest Aaron, just as it filled all the air around.[17]

Thomas Howard, in his explication of the novel, notes, "Every time we find Williams referring to hands in this story we may be sure that he wants us to be conscious of the awesome freedom that we humans have to choose, and hence to determine our destiny. Shall we wreck, or shall we build? What do our hands reveal about us?"[18]

Cockburn is pithier, as usual, but in a song written shortly after discovering Williams, he also employs the image of hands as instruments of salvation that is evocative of the scene above, substituting a "diamond wind" for Williams' "aureate splendour":

At the feast of fools,
people's hands weave light.

There is a diamond wind
flowering in the darkest night.[19]

Over the years, we see a progression in Cockburn's treatment of Exchange, from the grudging willingness to be helped in 1983's "The Strong One," to the acknowledgement of reciprocity in 1988's "The Gift." But thereafter, Cockburn's focus seems to be simply on generosity, without any expectation of return. In his 1996 updated setting of the 23rd Psalm, "Strange Waters," he sings,

Seen a forest in flames right down to the road,
burned in love till I've seen my heart explode...
Some will run and some will stand,
everything is bullshit but the open hand.
You've been leading me
beside strange waters.[20]

When an interviewer later asked him, "What is this open-handedness you're referring to?" Cockburn replied, "I could have said open heart. It's openness, period, the willingness to share what you have and to accept what others are willing to share with you, and what God or the universe is willing to share with you, and you back." This generosity becomes even more pronounced on 1999's "When You Give it Away":

Deep in the city of the saints and fools,
pearls before pigs and dung become jewels.
I sit down with tigers, I sit down with lambs,
none of them know who exactly I am.
I've got this thing in my heart
I must give you today.
It only lives when you
give it away.[21]

On that same album, Cockburn continues to talk about giving with no thought of receiving, but this time the Gift is presented in a poignant package, seeing and acknowledging the darkness and difficulty of another, and digging deep into one's own physical and spiritual resources in order to help, the very definition of "Substituted Love":

I've been scraping little shavings off my ration of light,
and I've formed it into a ball, and each time I pack a bit more onto it.
I make a bowl of my hands and I scoop it from its secret cache
under a loose board in the floor.
And I blow across it and I send it to you
against those moments when
the darkness blows under your door.
Isn't that what friends are for?[22]

---

1. Somehow, a typo has crept into this most famous of passages from *DiH.* Williams' original MS reads "rest of us" not "best of us." Attested to by Sarah Thompson in an as-yet unpublished annotated edition of *DiH.*
2. *DiH,* 91–92.
3. *Ibid.,* 97.
4. Galatians 4:2
5. *He Came Down from Heaven,* 82–83.
6. "Bors to Elayne: On the King's Coins," *Taliessin Through Logres,* 62–63.
7. Regina Baümer and Michael Plattig, "Desert Fathers and Spiritual Direction," in *Presence: An International Journal of Spiritual Direction* (Summer 2001).
8. *He Came Down from Heaven,* 81, 123.
9. *Ibid.,* 84–85.
10. "Love Loves You, Too," *D2H.*
11. "The Charity of Night," *CoN.*
12. "Songwriting Workshop, pt. 2," 1998 Festival of Faith and Writing Conference, Lab Theatre, Calvin College. 4 April 1998.
13. "The Redeemed City," *Image of the City,* 108.
14. "The Strong One," *ICF.*
15. *DiH,* 104.
16. "The Gift," *BiC.*
17. *GT,* 183–184.

18. Howard, 127.
19. "Feast of Fools," *FAO.*
20. "Strange Waters," *CoN.*
21. "When You Give It Away," *BNO.*
22. "Isn't That What Friends Are For?" *BNO.*

6
DAMNATION & SALVATION

DAMNATION: THE REJECTION OF CO-INHERENCE

Perhaps the most harrowing portrait in any of Williams' novels is that of Lawrence Wentworth in *Descent into Hell*. He is an historian, and at every turn of the novel we see him make choices in which he rejects communion with others and isolates himself more and more. Williams writes of him,

> The son of Adam [Wentworth] waited. He felt, coming over that vast form, that Hill of the dead and of the living, but to him only the mass of matter from which his perfect satisfaction was to approach, a road, a road up which a shape, no longer vast, was now coming; a shape he distrusted before he discerned it. It was coming slowly, over the mass of the Adam, a man, a poor ragged sick man. The dead man, walking in his own quiet world, knew nothing of the eyes to which his death-day walk was shown, nor of the anger with which he was seen. Wentworth saw him, and grew demented; was he to miss and be mocked again? what shape was this, and there? He sprang forward and up, to drive it away, to curse it lest it

> interpolated its horrid need between himself and his perfection. He would not have it: no canvassers, no hawkers, no tramps. He shouted angrily, making gestures; it offended him; it belonged to the City, and he would not have a City—no City, no circulars, no beggars. No; no; no. No people but his, no loves but his.[1]

In Williams' theology, heaven is community because God *is* a community. Those in heaven see that everything and everyone is connected to and dependent on everything and everyone else. Heaven is embracing the fact of the co-inherent nature of Reality, giving our willing assent to it, and actively participating in it. Williams writes, "The glory of God is in facts. The almost incredible nature of things is that there is no fact which is not in His glory. This is the great inclusion which makes the City."[2] God's hope for us is that we participate with a glad heart in the whole, for the good of the whole.

Contrary to this, hell is the rejection of community, of co-inherence. Hell is the refusal to acknowledge our finitude and accept help, to rely on others or make ourselves available for their support and assistance. Martin Luther refers to this as a soul that is *incurvatus in se*, turned in on itself. To enter hell is to choose the illusion of separateness and isolation over the reality of interdependence. The Zoroastrian name for hell is telling: "the House of the Lie." A soul who chooses hell cuts itself off from communion with other beings, retreating into a world of their own making, focused entirely on the self. Cockburn describes this state of alienation in a song that images the flight from human community and mutuality and responsibility as a locomotive plunging into the dark:

Not a knife throw from here you can hear the night train passing.
That's the sound somebody makes when they're getting away,
leaving next week's hanging jury far behind them,
prisoner only of the choices they've made.

Night train.

Ice cube in a dark drink shines like starlight.
The moon is floating somewhere out at sea.
I'm an island in the blur of noise and color:
Alcatraz, St. Helena, Patmos, and the Chateau D'If.
Night train.

And everyone's an island edged with sand,
a temporary refuge where somebody else can stand,
'til the sea that binds us like the forced tide of a blood oath
will wear it down—dissolve it—recombine it.

Anyone can die here, they do it every day.
It doesn't take much effort, though it goes against the grain.
And the ultimate forgetfulness of violence
sweeps the landscape like a headlight of a train.
Night train...

And in the absence of a vision there are nightmares,
and in the absence of compassion there is cancer,
whose banner waves over palaces and mean streets,
and the rhythm of the night train is a mantra.[3]

Cockburn unpacks the meaning of this song in his autobiography, acknowledging Williams' theology directly:

> No man is an island. At the subatomic level we are as connected to each other, and to everything else, as if we all share organs. At this level, prayer, as a focusing of spiritual energy, has tremendous power. This is where we find Charles Williams's Co-inherence, the unified Divine presence that exists in each other. To the extent that we are not conscious of that, we are islands. We live in the illusion of separateness. The islands in the song are

not vacation spots. Alcatraz, St. Helena, Patmos, and the Château d'If are all prison islands.[4]

We see a vivid portrayal of precisely this kind of self-exile in Williams' novel *Descent into Hell.* The title refers to Wentworth's spiritual journey as he progressively cuts himself off from others, moving into "night train" territory. In contrast to his descent, we see the ascent into heaven of Pauline Anstruther, who learns to trust and open herself to others, to rely on them and to offer them her help in return. As Howard describes it, "The two main characters go in opposite directions, the one towards solitude, wrath, ennui, and oblivion; and the other towards coinherence, joy, fullness, and liberty."[5]

Williams sums up the choice this way: "There is but one dichotomy: that between those who acknowledge that they live from the life of others, including their enemies, and those who do not."[6] Cockburn agrees, singing,

Here we are, faced with choice:
shutters and walls or open embrace.
Like it or not, the human race
is us all.[7]

Yet we must be careful not to "blame the victim." While Evangelical Christianity has a tendency to emphasize individual salvation, Catholic and Orthodox members of the Christian family have always emphasized their corporate nature. Meanwhile, mainline Protestants often come down somewhere in the middle, conceding both corporate and individual factors at play. As an Anglican, Williams acknowledges that the problem has corporate, communal, even systemic aspects. In an essay called "Natural Goodness" he wrote about

> ...the chosen catastrophe which we call the Fall. Whether in that state in which mankind was, the Fall was a single act of a single

> soul, or the simultaneous act of all souls, this is not the place to discuss. It is, I suppose, possible (since it is to be believed that every human creature sins) that in some way every human nature sinned at once; that the whole web was at once and everywhere ruined. That is irrelevant to the fact that, however it happened, it certainly happened.[8]

We all share in the common "sickness" of sin—a theology found in the early church fathers, and commonly referred to as the "medical model" of Christianity today. Cockburn utters a heartbreaking prayer expressing a cosmic pandemic from which everyone suffers (and which we inflict on creation):

Way out on the rim of the galaxy,
the gifts of the Lord lie torn.
Into whose charge the gifts were given
have made it a curse for so many to be born.
This is my trouble—
these were my fathers.
So how am I supposed to feel?
Way out on the rim of the broken wheel...

You and me—we are the break in the broken wheel,
bleeding wound that will not heal.
Lord, spit on our eyes so we can see
how to wake up from this tragedy.[9]

There is a both/and-ness to this theology. The wheel is broken, *and* individual souls have agency. We can accede to brokenness and allow ourselves to be further alienated from the whole, or we can turn (the word used in the New Testament is *metanoia*, "change of heart") and seek reintegration with others, with God, with creation—with the whole. As Williams wrote,

> It is not for us to make a division; that power our Lord explicitly reserved to Himself. If we insist on it, we can, in His final judgement, be separated. That is hell. But only our selves can put us there, and we cannot put others there.[10]

Nor will God put us there. He may, as Williams asserts, reserve that power explicitly to himself, but he permits us our own choices. If we choose to go our own way, he may woo us, but he will not drag us back into community by force. Coercion is not in God's nature. In every one of Williams' novels, we see this truth play out on the stage of his dramas. Every one of his characters—protagonists and antagonists alike—get exactly what they really want, deep in their heart of hearts.

In *All Hallows' Eve*, for example, when we first meet Lester, we infer that she is a self-centered person, because when she dies, she finds herself stranded in a version of London completely devoid of people. As Thomas Howard notes, "It is as though it is said to her, There: you wanted, really, a world with no people in it (they are such bores). Well, here it is."[11]

Cockburn affirms this agency regarding our own fate in his 1978 song, "Feast of Fools":

At the feast of fools,
everybody has a voice.
Nobody goes to the bottom
except by their own choice.[12]

What Williams so helpfully reveals in his novels is that salvation and damnation rarely come in huge, dramatic acts, but are usually the result of the accumulation of tiny choices. In an essay, he writes, "...all the qualities and all the glories of that human creation were not in one moment changed to a state of hell. So much the decree of process itself forbade. The end might be inevitable, but it had to be gradual."[13]

Gradual—and cumulative. If you wake up and smoke a

cigarette every morning for 1000 days, what are you likely to do on day 1001? Exactly the same. This is what Theravada Buddhists call *karma*, and what moral theologians call the cultivation of virtue (or vice, as the case may be). We choose the kind of people we want to become in every minuscule choice. And so, in fact, there are no insignificant choices. This "snowballing" effect of sin, separation, and isolation is poignantly described by Cockburn, while once more invoking the "medical model"[14] of Christianity:

So I find out what the luxury of hate is:
as exciting maybe as doing the dishes.
Face toward window—light received.

You get bigger as you go.
No one told me—I just know.
Bales of memory like boats in tow.
You get bigger as you go.

You get bigger as you go.
Telephone snarls "don't touch me."
You move in waves like the midnight blues.
You vector of this weird dis-ease.[15]

But in Williams' theology, damnation is never absolute, nor final, nor eternal. The further one walks in any one direction, the easier it is to keep on walking in that direction. And yet...it is always possible to turn around.

SALVATION: ASSENT TO CO-INHERENCE AND THE RESTORATION OF COMMUNION

Hidden among Williams' "deep cuts" is a fascinating atonement theory. In his essay, "Natural Goodness," he asserts, "The definition of the Fall is that man determined to know good as evil."[16] In

He Came Down from Heaven, he applies this theory to the Garden of Eden myth:

> The change in knowledge is indicated by one detail. The tale presents the Adam as naked, and in a state of enjoyment of being naked. It was part of their good; they had delight in their physical natures. There is no suggestion that they had not a delight in their sexual natures and relationship. They had about them a free candour, and that candour of joy was a part of their good. They were not ashamed. They then insisted on knowing good as evil; and they did. They knew that candour as undesirable; they experienced shame.[17]

We have been calling "good" "evil" ever since, making the holiness of the body an object of despite, proclaiming the material world to be inferior to the spiritual, twisting the fact of God's ardor into the lie of God's enmity, and in every other way forsaking the goodness of creation with slanderous psychologies, ideologies, and theologies. Williams writes, "The contradiction in the nature of man is thus completely established. He knows good, and he knows good as evil. These two capacities will always be present in him; his love will always be twisted with anti-love, with anger, with spite, with jealousy, with alien desires."[18]

This impulse to twist good into evil is a product of the House of the Lie, and it does violence to the Whole. Its wrath and wreckage multiply, infecting and affecting everyone, bringing cumulative, compounding suffering in its wake. Williams writes, "But if the good, which was whole, was to be known as evil, then process must be known as evil; that is, the process must be to a living death. The end would be hell."[19]

But in the presence of the Real, no lie can ultimately stand. The Omnipotence, in its wisdom, set forth to undo this damage. If the Fall came about by calling what is good "evil," then redemption must come about by seeing evil as an ultimate good (a shift in perspective) and approaching evil and suffering as occasions to bring about what is good (a shift in behavior). The archetype—or to use Williams' word, the *pattern*—for this transformation is the crucifixion, when God (in Jesus) took an evil act (persecution, torture, and murder) and used it as an occasion for good (forgiveness, the bearing of others' burdens, and resurrection). As Williams explained:

> It is the name now given to the heavenly knowledge of the evil of earth; evil is known as an occasion of good, that is, of love. It has been always so known on the side of heaven, but now it can be so known on the side of earth also. Pardon, or reconciliation, was not defined by the prophets as more than oblivion, for in time mankind had not experienced that reconciliation. Nor could mankind, by itself, ever reach it, for mankind by itself could not endure the results of its choice, the total deprivation of good, and yet recover joyous awareness of good. What mankind could not do, manhood did, and a manhood which was at the disposal of all men and women. It was therefore possible now for mankind itself to know evil as an occasion of heavenly love.[20]

Cockburn sums this up with pith and clarity when he sings:

Around every evil there gathers love —
bombs aren't the only things that fall from above.[21]

In Williams' novels, we see this shift in both perspective and behavior played out. In *War in Heaven*, after the climax sees the villain flee, Lionel is talking with Prester John (the stranger):

> ...the stranger said to Lionel, "Yet he may escape."
>
> Lionel looked up. "Oh, yes," he said vaguely, though he felt the fantasy, as he stood alone with the other, take sharp form within his mind. "Oh, yes—that, but something awaits him surely of ruin and of despair."

> "It may be," the stranger said, "but perhaps a happy ruin and a fortunate despair. These things are not evil in themselves, and I think you fear them overmuch."[22]

This is an allusion to *felix culpa* ("happy fault" or "fortunate sin"), taken from the Tridentine Easter Vigil: "O happy fault that earned for us so great, so glorious a Redeemer."[23] As Augustine explained the concept, "For God judged it better to bring good out of evil than not to permit any evil to exist."[24] Williams certainly knew his Augustine, but it is equally likely that his atonement theory has its roots in Milton's *Paradise Lost*, wherein Adam, finally understanding the magnitude and glory of God's plan, exclaims,

> O goodness infinite, goodness immense!
> That all this good of evil shall produce,
> And evil turn to good; more wonderful
> Then that which by creation first brought forth
> Light out of darkness! full of doubt I stand,
> Whether I should repent me now of sin
> By mee done and occasiond, or rejoyce
> Much more, that much more good thereof shall spring,
> To God more glory, more good will to Men
> From God, and over wrauth grace shall abound.[25]

Williams quotes one of his favorite mystics, Julian of Norwich, saying, "Every sin shall have worship in heaven."[26] This is a shocking statement, but elsewhere Julian explains in more measured terms: "Sin is behovely, but all shall be well, and all shall be well, and all manner of things shall be well."[27] "Behovely" is an archaic Middle English word meaning "useful," "beneficial," or "necessary."

Williams is asserting that the web of co-inherence must be ripped in order for love to transcend, transform, and heal the tear. If there is no occasion for evil, then there is no occasion for love, either. Tolkien called such events "eucatastrophes"—disastrous events which bring about a blessed end.[28] Cockburn creates a vivid image of a eucatastrophic event in the title of his song, "Shipwrecked at the Stable Door."

Cockburn doesn't often get into the theological weeds on this topic, so the shift in perspective is not evident in his lyrics, but as with Williams' novels, we do see it clearly in his reports of peoples' behavior. Perhaps the most luminous example of this in all of Cockburn's repertoire is "Peggy's Kitchen Wall." As he often does in his songs, Cockburn is giving us a snapshot—or a short movie, rather—of something he actually witnessed. There has been an act of random violence (or at least, gross negligence) in his apartment building:

Crashing in the kitchen, noises in the hall.
Roll over and go back to sleep—it's just a dream, that's all.
So how come the window's broken, what caused the glass to fall?
And who put that bullet hole in Peggy's kitchen wall?

Police arrive—muddy up the floor,
dig out half the plaster—it's a .38 for sure.
Kick the neighbour's door in, saying, "Better tell it all—
who put that bullet hole in Peggy's kitchen wall?"

But what results from this violent act is unexpected—around this evil gathers love as his community comes together:

Blaster on the back porch, shaking up the lane.
They're drinking gin and joking—laughter falling down like rain.
Everybody wears a halo, never saw nothing at all.
So who put that bullet hole in Peggy's kitchen wall?

What is most unexpected—and unexpectedly charming—about this portrayal is the moral complexity of Cockburn's community. Yes, the incident brings them together, but no one is forthcoming with any information. The characters in Williams' novels are likewise morally ambiguous. Bit by bit, we see deeply flawed characters edge toward salvation, sometimes in spite of themselves. In *All Hallows' Eve*, for example, the novel opens with Lester Furnival, a young, newly married woman who finds herself on Westminster Bridge in a completely silent, inexplicably depopulated London. She is dead, but does not yet know she is dead. As we get to know her, we see that she is vain, self-obsessed, and has a cruel streak. And yet here, at the very beginning, moments after she has died, Williams shows us that the seeds of her salvation are already planted and ready to bud forth:

> ...somewhere in her there was a small desire to see someone—a woman reading, children playing, a man listening to the wireless; something of that humanity which must be near, but of which on that lonely bridge she could feel nothing.[29]

That desire for connection with another human being is enough for her to take one step in the direction of communion, community, co-inherence. And then presently another, until she is well on her way to restoration, and aiding in the restoration of others.

Williams is not of the Calvinistic "total depravity" school of Christianity. Life—including death, faith, and salvation—is never simple; it is always a messy affair. The seeds of goodness are always present, even in the most hardened sinner; and the seeds of evil are also at hand, even in the most reverend saint. Cockburn refers to this as "the burden of the angel/beast."[30] In an essay titled "Natural Goodness," Williams explains:

> [Man's] blood might be tainted, but the source from which it sprang was still the same. His natural life was still, and is now, a disordered pattern of the only pattern, a confused type of the one original; it is full still of glory and of peace, as well as of bloodshed and despair. It contends within itself. The most

> extreme goodness may be found in it and asserted of it —so long as the absolute invalidity of it apart from the new life is also declared.[31]

Cockburn echoes a sense of that moral complexity when he sings,

> *So many people, so lost, you feel sorry.*
> *But too much pathos just makes you angry.*
> *And even though I know who loves me*
> *I'm not that much less lost.*[32]

But that very complexity works in our favor, for Love's pursuit of us is never abandoned, either in this life or the next. We can *always* turn around (*metanoia*). And yet, even in our restoration there is complexity, as demonstrated by the risen Christ, newly restored to wholeness, but who nevertheless showed Thomas and the other disciples the wounds in his hands and side. Williams writes,

> Death is an outrage, a necessary outrage, upon a unity. We must accept it, as we must accept, for ourselves or for others, many another outrage. But it has been regarded, from the beginning, as an unnatural thing, a separation in the unseparate... There is, there, no more rule "in unity itself."
>
> Except by the restoration of the union. The high doctrine of the physical Resurrection restores to mankind the unity of which it had been deprived. The new union can hardly be scarless; the original Unity, so again unified, must bear the marks of its wounds—as indeed it does: say, to name but one, of the spear-thrust in the side. Yet it is said that this, and the others, are "glorified." They wear a double radiance—of the original and of the renovation.[33]

Just as in Taoism, yin contains the seed of yang and yang

contains the seed of yin, so brokenness and wholeness interpenetrate, nothing can be excluded from Oneness, everything participates in co-inherence—like it or not, want it or not, know it or not.

---

1. *DiH,* 81.
2. "The Redeemed City," *Image of the City*, 110.
3. "Night Train," *CoN.*
4. Cockburn, 414–415.
5. Howard, 182.
6. "Anthropotokos," *Image of the City*, 113.
7. "Us All," *OSOM*.
8. "Natural Goodness," *Image of the City*, 77.
9. "Broken Wheel," *ICF.*
10. "The Way of Exchange," *Image of the City*, 153.
11. Howard, 154.
12. "Feast of Fools," *FAO*.
13. "Natural Goodness," *Image of the City*, 77.
14. The Medical Model of Christianity is mentioned by Williams as well. In his poem, "House-hunting," he writes: "Or you with Love being mightily content, / The sickness done which your light present sin / Shall at that change bring on till, pale and thin, / You are renewed with heavenly nourishment,— / That hot and scarfing malady quite spent, / Shall you, some household of his choice within, / With him new travel and new toil begin, / Nor glance at dogs on their own mischief bent?" *Divorce*, 29.
15. "You Get Bigger as You Go," *HU.*
16. "Natural Goodness," *Image of the City,* 77.
17. *He Came Down from Heaven,* 18–19.
18. *Ibid.*, 20.
19. "Natural Goodness," *Image of the City*, 77.
20. *He Came Down from Heaven,* 55.
21. "Where the Death Squad Lives," *BiC.*
22. *WiH*, 247–248.
23. *Catholic Encyclopedia*, "Exultet."
24. Augustine, *Enchiridion*, viii.
25. Milton, John. *Paradise Lost*, book XII, lines 469–478.
26. "The Redeemed City," *Image of the City*, 109; *Revelations of Divine Love,* chap. 38.
27. Julian of Norwich. *Revelations of Divine Love*, long text, chap. 27.
28. "But the 'consolation' of fairy-stories has another aspect than the imaginative satisfaction of ancient desires. Far more important is the Consolation of the Happy Ending. Almost I would venture to assert that all complete fairy-stories must have it. At least I would say that Tragedy is the true form of

Drama, its highest function; but the oppositive is true of Fairy-story. Since we do not appear to possess a word that expresses this opposite—I will call it *Eucatastrophe*. The *eucatastrophic* tale is the true form of fairy-tale, and its highest function... The consolation of fairy-stories, the joy of the happy ending: or more correctly of the good catastrophe, the sudden joyous 'turn' (for there is no true end to any fairy-tale): this joy, which is one of the things which fairy-tales can produce supremely well, is not essentially 'escapist,' nor 'fugitive.' In its fairy-tale—or otherworld—setting, it is a sudden and miraculous grace: never to be counted on to recur. It does not deny the existence of *dyscatastrophe*, of sorrow and failure: the possibility of these is necessary to the joy of deliverance; it denies (in the face of much evidence, if you will) universal final defeat and in so far is *evangelium*, giving a fleeting glimpse of Joy, Joy beyond the walls of the world, poignant as grief... I would venture to say that approaching the Christian Story from this direction, it has long been my feeling (a joyous feeling) that God redeemed the corrupt making-creatures, men, in a way fitting to this aspect, as to others, of their strange nature. The Gospels contain a fairy-story... The Birth of Christ is the eucatastrophe of Man's history. The Resurrection is the eucatastrophe of the story of the Incarnation... There is no tale ever told that men would rather find was true..." Tolkien, 81.

29. *AHE*, 3.
30. "Burden of the Angel/Beast," *D2H*.
31. "Natural Goodness," *Image of the City*, 78.
32. "Civilization and Its Discontents," *TWN*.
33. "The Redeemed City," *Image of the City*, 104.

PART II
THE IMAGES

Truth did not come into the world naked,
but through symbols and images.
—Gospel of Philip, 59

7
THE IMPORTANCE OF IMAGES

When comparing Williams' writings and Cockburn's lyrics what is striking is a similar emphasis on images. Both are fiercely visual writers, and both cast images one after another that suggest something grander than any one image can evoke. C. S. Lewis said of Williams' poetry, "He is in one way full of images: but where he is most himself each image is no sooner suggested than it fades—or, dare I say? *brightens*—into something invisible and intangible."[1]

Take, for example, this excerpt from Williams' "Taliessin in the School of the Poets,"

> *Tendebantque manus*—there[2]
>   in the broad Phœbeian ground
> they saw the macrocosm drawn;
> they heard the universal sigh
> in the balance of changing levels
>   and complemented sound.
>
> Infinite patterns opened
>   in the sovereign's chair's mass;
> but the crowned form of anatomized man,

bones, nerves, sinews,
the diagram of the style of the Logos,
rose in the crimson brass.[3]

Here Williams is stacking images almost willy-nilly, so it is hard to discern exactly what any of it means. Cockburn is rarely this opaque, but he, too, stacks images one atop the other. In one of his most well-known songs, he sings,

Silver scales flash bright and fade
in reeds along the shore.
Like a pearl in a sea of liquid jade,
his ship comes shining.
Like a crystal swan in a sky of suns,
his ship comes shining.[4]

He is likewise image-dense and eloquent when describing the seedier side of the world:

The skin around every city looks the same,
miles of flat neon spelling well-known names:
USED TRUCKS—
DIRTY DONUTS—
YOU YOU'RE THE ONE,
fat wheeled cars squeal into the sun.

Radio speakers gargle top-40 trash,
muzak soundtrack to slow collapse.
Planet engines pulsate in sidereal time.
If you listen close you can hear the whine.[5]

But more important than technique is the philosophy behind these visions—not only what they mean, but how they mean it. Anne Ridley, describing Williams' work, wrote, "These images, once known, become for us one of the means by which we touch reality."[6] Far from being an impressionistic grab bag of unrelated icons, their poetic juxtaposition point beyond themselves to something infinitely more sublime. St. Paul asserted as much in his letter to the Christians at Rome: "Ever since the creation of the world God's eternal power and divine nature, invisible though they are, have been seen and understood through the things God has made."[7]

We are, of course, talking about symbols, but not in the anemic sense that we have come to think of them. "Symbol" comes from the Greek *συμβάλλω*, "I throw together," and in ancient literature it suggests not just a mental connection, but an ontological one as well. As Plato asserted in *Phaedo*, "If anything else is beautiful besides Beauty itself, it is beautiful for no other reason than that it participates in that Beauty and likewise in all cases."[8]

This "participation" acknowledges the worth of the Signifier in its own right, even as it mediates communion with the larger reality Signified. It is for this reason that Williams prefers the word "image" to "symbol." In his introduction to *The Figure of Beatrice*, he notes that Coleridge asserted that "a symbol must have three characteristics (i) it must exist in itself, (ii) it must derive from something greater than itself, (iii) it must represent in itself that greatness from which it derives." He continues, "It seems to me doubtful if the word symbol nowadays sufficiently expresses the vivid existence of the lesser thing."[9]

This is truly The Way of Affirmation, since unlike the dualistic tendency to honor only "the things above," due honor is given as well to the Signifier—no matter how humble, it is still holy, not only by its association with the Signified, but because of the inherent goodness of all creation and the joy God takes in the Signifier itself. Writing about the sacraments, Thomas Aquinas admits they are "God's gracious concession to man's regrettably sensuous nature." Yet according to Gunnar Urang, Williams embraces the "classical" theology of Irenaeus, that the sacraments are "symbols of the ultimate unity of nature and grace."[10] At the same time, as Williams was fond of saying, "The vision is more than the prince."[11] All truth is paradoxical, and holding the value of the Signifier and the Signified in tension is key to their power.

This "participation" of the symbol in the reality to which it points is, for Williams, no doubt traceable to the occult philosophy of the FRC (and the Golden Dawn), which held that everything in heaven and earth is intimately connected, and indeed, intertwined. Magicians assemble Tables of Correspondences in an attempt to map out these connections, so that by means of them one's magical intention can become more potent. For instance, knowing that there is a correspondence between the Hebrew letter Bet, the number 2, the Magician card of the tarot, the motion "up" in the Kabbalistic Tree of Life, the note E natural, the planet Mercury, and the colors yellow and purple can help a magician construct a ritual that makes use of the natural yet unseen "links" between these things toward a more effective assertion of the magician's will.[12]

According to Glen Cavaliero, Williams was also influenced by the work of Arthur Machen (1863–1947), a novelist and mystic who pioneered precisely the kind of "occult thrillers" that Williams sought to produce. Cavaliero writes, "Machen's outlook is a kind of unsystematized Neo-Platonism; and throughout his writing career he was a vociferous champion of that literature which was based on what he designated 'ecstasy,' by which he means the realisation of [an] underlying or overarching world of spiritual reality."[13] It seems Williams adopted this nomenclature for himself in his first novel, *Shadows of Ecstasy*. In Williams' hands, the smallest of things can be shadows—or indications—of the largest realities.

In that first novel, as the character of Sir Bernard is taking a quiet moment for himself, he reflects on "an insane political hot-gospeller in Hyde Park, Caithness vestmented in an ecclesiastical ceremony, the antique faces of the Jews in the crude reproductions of the [news]papers, a look in Philip's eyes as he watched Rosamond, the silly raucous voices of the crowd in the streets..."[14]

—all of these, he realizes, are indicators of larger realities. The novel's ambiguous hero/antihero Considine comments, "a kiss also is but the shadow of ecstasy."[15] If these indicators seem to be insignificant, so much the better for Williams' purpose. As Thomas Howard notes about another of the novels, "The whole point in every flick of every wrist in the whole story is precisely that everything means everything. Glory and mystery lie at our elbow all the time."[16]

In his lyrics, Cockburn employs the same meaning-dense perspective. He sings,

There's a rainbow shining in a bead of spittle,
falling diamonds in rattling rain.
Light flexed on moving muscle,
I stand here dazzled with my heart in flames
at this world of wonders...[17]

Instead of "shadows of ecstasy," however, Cockburn opts for the phrase, "rumours of glory," which he puts to fine use in his song of that name:

Above the dark town,
after the sun's gone down,
two vapour trails cross the sky,
catching the day's last slow goodbye.
Black skyline looks rich as velvet,
something is shining
like gold but better—
rumours of glory.[18]

The "two vapour trails" recalls Constantine's vision of the cross in the sky, with the attendant voice commanding him to conquer by that sign, but it seems Cockburn has something more benign in mind. In a liner note, Cockburn notes simply, "Dusk in Manhattan—streets filled and emptied as people rushed from office to subway. All those hearts, and a cross in the icy sky. Image upon image, adding up to more than the sum of their parts..."[19]

Williams also used the word "rumour" to describe indications of transcendent reality. In his first book of poetry, *The Silver Stair*, he wrote:

> Rumour: the loves that once possessed my days
> Begin to whisper messages of thee.
> They, while in conscious shame I stand at, gaze
> Upon the frontiers of thy royalty,
> Sound trumpets in thy heart's most secret ways
> And shake the portals unbeheld of me.[20]

Being poets, neither Cockburn nor Williams are always clear about what their signifiers are pointing to, exactly. That ambiguity is fecund, giving rise to previously unconscious connections that reveal delightful correspondences that are sometimes more felt than understood. Of the time when he wrote "Rumours of Glory," Cockburn noted, "There's a certain style of song that started to show up, and became more typical of my songwriting through that period, which is a kind of documentary-style thing, structured like a little movie...where you try and set up these little scenes that relate to each other but where you don't have to explain the relationship but there's an impression that's created out of it that adds up to something."[21]

Williams describes much the same in a blurb about *Taliessin through Logres*: "The poems do not so much tell a story or describe a process as express states or principles of experience. The names and incidents of the Arthurian myth are taken as starting-points for investigation and statement on common and profound experience."[22]

Williams summed up his hope that readers would benefit from these "shadows" and "rumors" in a prayer he composed for a marriage ceremony:

God, who by the teaching of holy doctors hast called us in all images and patterns to the unimaginable peace of goodwill: Grant that we may so study felicity with our minds that we may attain it in our lives: Who in the Triune Mystery are the perfect and only Godhead. Amen.[23]

---

1. Ridler, lxvii.
2. An allusion to Virgil, "tendebantque manus ripae ulterioris amore" translates to "and they were reaching out their hands with love for the further shore." This line describes the souls of the dead reaching out to cross the river Styx in the underworld. *Aeneid*, Book VI.
3. *Taliessin Through Logres,* 48.
4. "All the Diamonds in the World," *SST.*
5. "Silver Wheels," *IFD.*
6. Ridler, lxxi.
7. Romans 1:20
8. Plato, *Phaedo,* 100c.
9. *Figure of Beatrice*, 7.
10. Urang, 81.
11. Ridler, xliv.
12. Table of "Magical Correspondences" compiled by Bill Heidrick, https://www.billheidrick.com/works/tarottbl.htm
13. Cavaliero, 55.
14. *SoE*, 97.
15. *Ibid.,* 153.
16. Howard, 136.
17. "World of Wonders," *WoW*.
18. "Rumours of Glory," *HU.*
19. From the liner notes of *Greatest Hits (1970–2020).*
20. *Silver Stair*, 27.
21. From "Bruce Cockburn: A Burning Light and All the Rest" by William Ruhlmann, *Goldmine* magazine, 3 April 1992.
22. Quoted by Ridler, lxiv–lxv.
23. *Image of the City,* 195.

8

THE IMAGE OF THE CITY

In *All Hallows' Eve*, Williams gives us an early scene that is hard to shake. Richard has gone to visit his friend Jonathan, an artist, who is showing him two of his most recent paintings.

> "Over here," Jonathan said, and took his friend round to the other side of the room. A second easel was standing back to back with the first, also holding a canvas, but this uncovered. Richard set himself to look at it.
>
> It was of a part of London after a raid—he thought, of the City proper, for a shape on the right reminded him dimly of St. Paul's. At the back were a few houses, but the rest of the painting was of a wide stretch of desolation. The time was late dawn; the sky was clear; the light came, it seemed at first, from the yet unrisen sun behind the single group of houses. The light was the most outstanding thing in the painting; presently, as Richard looked, it seemed to stand out from the painting, and almost to dominate the room itself. At least it so governed the painting that all other details and elements were contained within it. They floated in that imaginary light as the earth does

> in the sun's… All that massiveness of colour was led, by delicate gradations almost like the vibrations of light itself, towards the hidden sun; the eye encountered the gradations in their outward passage and moved inwards towards their source. It was then that the style of the painting came fully into its own. The spectator became convinced that the source of that light was not only in that hidden sun, as, localized, it certainly was. "Here lies the east; does not the day break here?" The day did, but the light did not. The eye, nearing that particular day, realized that it was leaving the whole fullness of the light behind. It was everywhere in the painting—concealed in houses and in their projected shadows, lying in ambush in the cathedral, opening in the rubble, vivid in the vividness of the sky. It would everywhere have burst through, had it not chosen rather to be shaped into forms, and to restrain and change its greatness in the colours of those lesser limits. It was universal, and lived.[1]

On the surface of things, "The City" refers to London, but in Williams' theology, London is but a shadow, a symbol, an image of co-inherence, of the interdependent oneness of all things. All cities serve this function for us—they are themselves the locus of interdependence for those who live there or travel through, and at the same time they point beyond themselves to a larger interconnected Reality, what theologians in the past called "the Kingdom of Heaven" and which theologians today have named "the Beloved Community." The ultimate image of this Community is the New Jerusalem of St. John's Apocalypse:

> And I saw the holy city, the new Jerusalem, coming down out of heaven from God, prepared as a bride adorned for her husband. And I heard a loud voice from the throne saying, "See, the home of God is among mortals. He will dwell with them; they will be his peoples, and God himself will be with them and be their God; he will wipe every tear from their eyes. Death will

> be no more; mourning and crying and pain will be no more, for the first things have passed away." And the one who was seated on the throne said, "See, I am making all things new." ...I saw no temple in the city, for its temple is the Lord God the Almighty and the Lamb. And the city has no need of sun or moon to shine on it, for the glory of God is its light, and its lamp is the Lamb.[2]

This image is of what Williams called, "The Redeemed City," in which all of the woundedness, illness, and brokenness of our contemporary cities will participate in the eschatological healing of all things. Williams writes, "There is no final idea for us [Christians] but the glory of God in the redeemed and universal union —call it Man or the Church or the City... The Re-creation [of] the original creation...was presented to us, in the Apocalypse, under the image of a City."[3] The City (or any of its shadow cities) are ideal representations of co-inherence precisely because it points to "the doctrine that no man lives to himself or indeed from himself. This is the doctrine common to nature and grace."[4]

The present and future cities co-inhere, in Williams' view, the former imperfect (but potent) images of the latter. He gives us a glimpse of this through Lester's experience in *All Hallow's Eve*. Early in the novel, Lester discovers that she is dead, but as she begins to recognize her need for others (and their need of her), her perspective begins to shift:

> Not only space but time spread out around her as she went. She saw a glowing and glimmering City, of which the life was visible as a roseal wonder within. The streets of it were first the streets of to-day, full of the business of to-day—shops, transport, men and women... The dreadful silence she had known after death was no longer there; the faint sound of traffic, so common but oh so uncommon, came to her. It was London known again and anew. Then, gently opening, she saw among those streets other streets. She had seen them in pictures, but now she did not think

> of pictures, for these were certainly the streets themselves—another London, say—other Londons, into which her own London opened or with which it was intermingled. No thought of confusion crossed her mind; it was all very greatly ordered, and when down a long street she saw, beyond the affairs of today, the movement of sedan chairs and ancient dresses, and beyond them again, right in the distance and yet very close to her, the sun shining on armour, and sometimes a high battlemented gate, it was no phantasmagoria of a dream but precise actuality. She was (though she did not find the phrase) looking along time. Once or twice she thought she saw other streets, unrecognizable, with odd buildings and men and women in strange clothes. But these were rare glimpses and less clear, as if the future of that City only occasionally showed... There around her lay not only London, but all cities—coincident yet each distinct; or else, in another mode, lying by each other as the districts of one city lie. She could, had the time and her occasions permitted, have gone to any she chose—any time and place that men had occupied or would occupy. There was no huge metropolis in which she would have been lost, and no single village which would itself have been lost in all that contemporaneous mass. In this City lay all—London and New York, Athens and Chicago, Paris and Rome and Jerusalem; it was that to which they led in the lives of their citizens.[5]

This is not an arid, transcendent reality, but one grounded in flesh and blood. Williams tells us, "The Holy Ghost moves us to be, by every means to which we are called, the Images of Christ, the types of that Original, in or out of the flesh. It is the intercourse of those free Images which is the union of the City."[6] Thus, our spiritual formation is directed toward active, conscious, and joyful participation in the whole. In the novel, Lester realizes this, too:

> When her time came, she would know what lay behind the high empty façades of her early experience of death; it was necessary that she should first have been compelled to linger among those façades, for till she had waited there and till she had known the first grace of a past redeemed into love, she could not bear even a passing glimpse of that civil vitality. For here citizenship meant relationship and knew it; its citizens lived new acts or lived the old at will. What on earth is only in the happiest moments of friendship or love was now normal.[7]

In Cockburn's lyrics, cities are rarely portrayed in such a positive light. His early music is grounded in late-1960s and early 1970s folk and rock, in which the hippie, "back-to-the-land" ideal is prominent, not unlike John Denver's approach in the U.S. Cockburn's first hit single, "Going to the Country," depicts a flight from the city to a bucolic getaway:

I can smell the grass growing in the field.
Wind in my hair tells me how it feels.
Farm house, silver roof flashing by.
Tractor-trailer truck says goodbye with a sigh.
And I'm going to the country...
sunshine smile on me.[8]

His lyrics often depict cities as places of danger and corruption. On that same debut album, he sings,

You know, these city towers,
jewels on the Serpent's crown,
twist the space between them
'til every eye is blinded.[9]

In 1978's "Outside a Broken Telephone Booth with Money in My Hand," he sings,

In the dead of night the city seems to break down into tribes.
You stare at too much concrete, you forget the earth's alive.[10]

The chorus of a song from his first album contains a particularly poignant petition:

Oh, Jesus, don't let Toronto take my song away.[11]

But a shift in his perspective comes about the time he first began reading Williams. This is also around the time of his divorce and his change of heart toward human community. In an interview, he said, "I embraced urban life at that point, which previously I'd been very suspicious of, and I made a point of kind of socializing myself in a very different way from how I had been before that point."[12] This led to a shift in his portrayal of cities. From that time forward, his work betrays a more balanced ambivalence toward cities, often weighing their ugliness and beauty in two hands. He holds these two in tension when he sings:

I turned on the TV war news,
just to look and wonder why.
Thunder crashed and red flash-flowers
bloomed a nightmare in the sky.

So I went down to the cafe,
just to string myself along.
On the way I found some riches—
played the jukebox, got this song.

While I sat there, a ragged man came—
bummed a coffee, talked awhile;
told me stories full of wonder—
left me laughing like a well-loved child.[13]

Williams felt that ambivalence, too. Like his character Stanhope, for which he was himself the pattern, he "was an optimist and hated it."[14] In *All Hallows' Eve* we read:

> The Thames was dirty and messy. Twigs, bits of paper and wood, cords, old boxes drifted on it. Yet to the new-eyed Lester it was not a depressing sight. The dirtiness of the water was, at that particular point, what it should be, and therefore, pleasant enough. The evacuations of the City had their place in the City; how else could the City be the City? Corruption (so to call it) was tolerable, even adequate and proper, even glorious. These things also were facts. They could not be forgotten or lost in fantasy; all that had been, was; all that was, was. A sodden mass of cardboard and paper drifted by, but the soddenness was itself a joy, for this was what happened, and all that happened, in this great material world, was good. The very heaviness of the heavy sky was a wonder, and the unutilitarian expectation of rain a delight.[15]

But just as Williams is capable of seeing both sides, Cockburn can also allow his ambivalence to give way to glory as he gives voice to a vision that is reminiscent of Jonathan's painting of the City:

...Through the joining and the parting,
the light goes on forever.
...Through the people and through the walls,
the light goes on forever.
Through who obeys and who does not,
through who gets rich and who gets caught,
the light goes on forever.
...Through the buildings and through the hills,
the light goes on forever.
Through the struggles and the games,
through the night's empty doorframes,

the light goes on forever.[16]

In a song from 1983's *The Trouble with Normal*, Cockburn places the vision of the City side-by-side with the reality of Toronto in his own version of "The Empire is the pattern; Logres the experiment":

We were lying in bliss,
love was cooling into sleep.
There was a dream on the horizon,
and a punch-up in the street.[17]

One final image will suffice to sum up Cockburn's Janus-like approach to urban life, one that combines the image of the City with the next metaphor we will examine:

River wrapped in concrete,
hills made to stand in chains.
Ain't the city pretty?
Shines like tear drops when it rains.

The city's hungry,
hear that rumblin' under ground.
My baby grabs me,
she starts to dance around.[18]

---

1. *AHE*, 23.
2. Rev. 21:2–5, 22–23.
3. "The Redeemed City," *Image of the City*, 102–104.
4. *Ibid.*, 104.
5. *AHE*, 161.
6. "The Redeemed City," *Image of the City*, 102.
7. *AHE*, 161.
8. "Going to the Country," *BC*.
9. "Man of a Thousand Faces," *BC*.
10. "Outside a Broken Telephone Booth with Money in My Hand," *FAO*.

11. "Thoughts On a Rainy Afternoon," *BC.*
12. "First Play and Q&A: Bruce Cockburn, Bone On Bone" by Andrea Warner, CBC Music.
13. "A Montreal Song," *FAO.*
14. *DiH,* 2.
15. *AHE,* 189–190.
16. "The Light Goes On Forever," bonus track on *ICF* reissue (2002).
17. "Going Up Against Chaos," *TWN.*
18. "The City is Hungry," *SOL.*

9
THE IMAGES OF THE DANCE & THE DANCING FOOL

THE DANCE

The image of the cosmos as a divinely ordered Dance goes back nearly as far as human writing. The Pyramid Texts of ancient Egypt employ the metaphor, as does the *Enūma Eliš*, the Babylonian creation myth preserved in cuneiform text on clay tablets.[1] In his *Timaeus*, Plato wrote,

> The Craftsman fashioned the stars mainly out of fire so that their divine race would be most luminous and beautiful to behold... To describe the choral dances of these same gods...and how at times they hide each other from us...to tell all this without visual models would be labor spent in vain.[2]

Philo, too, spoke of the "choral dances of the planets and fixed stars,"[3] but extends the image to embrace the whole of the created order:

> Is it not therefore likely, or indeed necessary that he who comes to the truly great city, the cosmos, and beholds hill and plain

> laden with animals and plants, the currents of rivers that rise in the country and those that are swollen with winter snow, the expanses of the seas, the temperateness of the air, the transition of the yearly seasons, then the sun and moon ruling day and night, and the other heavenly bodies, planets and fixed stars, and the revolutions and choral dances of the whole heaven, must gain an understanding of the Maker and Father and Ruler also?[4]

Christian writers picked up the metaphor and ran with it, beginning as early as the second-century Acts of John, where Jesus instructs his disciples in a circle dance, during which he sings,

> Grace is dancing.
> I wish to pipe.
> Dance, all of you.
> I wish to mourn, mourn all of you.
> Twelve is the number dancing on high.
> Ah, is it possible for the whole world to dance?[5]

That the Dance as a metaphor for divinely ordered creation should also lend itself to a depiction of co-inherence is not surprising, in that one way to translate the word *perichoresis* is "circle dance." It literally means "to move (or dance) around."[6] C.S. Lewis commented that "God is not a static *thing*' but 'almost a kind of *dance*,"[7] and used the image of a cosmic dance in the closing pages of *Perelandra*, a scene which owes much to Charles Williams' novel, *The Greater Trumps*.

In the opening scene of that novel, Williams introduces us to a family in mid-squabble. We meet Mr. Coningsby, his unflappable sister Sibyl, and his wayward daughter Nancy. When Nancy's fiancé Henry arrives for dinner, Coningsby muses—not kindly—on the young barrister's gypsy heritage. Mr. Coningsby had recently been bequeathed a collection of what he calls "playing cards," which turn out to be several historic decks of tarot cards, one of which turns out to be the ur-deck—the original deck from which all other tarot cards are derived. When Henry sees the cards from this deck, he declares them to be "very curious." When Nancy asks him why, he answers:

> "It's said that the shuffling of the cards is the earth, and the pattering of the cards is the rain, and the beating of the cards is the wind, and the pointing of the cards is the fire. That's of the four suits. But the Greater Trumps, it's said, are the meaning of all process and the measure of the everlasting dance."[8]

Later, at Nancy's prompting, Henry explains further:

> "Imagine that everything which exists takes part in the movement of a great dance—everything, the electrons, all growing and decaying things, all that seems alive and all that doesn't seem alive, men and beasts, trees and stones, everything that changes, and there is nothing anywhere that does not change. That change—that's what we know of the immortal dance; the law in the nature of things—that's the measure of the dance, why one thing changes swiftly and another slowly, why there is seeming accident and incalculable alteration, why men hate and love and grow hungry, and cities that have stood for centuries fall in a week, why the smallest wheel and the mightiest world revolve, why blood flows and the heart beats and the brain moves, why your body is poised on your ankles and the Himalaya are rooted in the earth—quick or slow, measurable or immeasurable, there is nothing at all anywhere but the dance. Imagine it—imagine it, see it all at once and in one! ...This is all that there is to learn; our happiest science guesses at the steps of a little of it. It's always perfect because it can't be anything else. It knows nothing of joy or grief; it's movement, quick as light, slow as the crumbling of a stone tomb in the jungle. If you cry, it's because the measure will have it so; if you laugh, it's because some gayer step demands it, not because you will. If you ache, the dance strains you; if you are healthy, the dance carries you. Medicine is the dance: law,

> religion, music, and poetry—all these are ways of telling ourselves the smallest motion that we've known for an instant before it utterly disappears in the unrepeatable process of *that*. O Nancy, see it, see it—that's the most we can do, to see something of it for the poor second before we die!"[9]

Cockburn captures well the magnitude of this cosmic vision in his song, "Everywhere Dance":

Moon of plenty, moon of mischance,
it'll be what you want but you can't stop the Dance.
Try to count the steps and they change while you stare.
And the translucent moon floats in waves of blue air.
And we cry out for grace to lay truth bare.
The Dance is the truth and it's everywhere.

Pas de deux *in stark silhouette,*
pulsing against a clear orange sunset.
As the distance shifts from skin unto skin,
look at how bodies shape the spaces they're in.
See the limbs slide smooth through unresisting air.
The Dance is the truth and it's everywhere.

In grains of sand and galaxies,
in plasma flow and rain in trees;
in the sepia swell of silted-up surf;
in the ebb and the flow of dying and birth;
in wounded streets and whispered prayer,
the Dance is the truth and it's everywhere.[10]

The Dance as a metaphor for co-inherence works better if your understanding of "dancing" is closer to a cotillion than a shindig or what one used to see on American Bandstand. This kind of dance has rules, order, structure, and requires people to know the moves so that the dance proceeds with a harmony

Confucius would have envied—this is not a chaotic free-for-all, it is choreography. It is possible to be out of step. It is possible to learn the steps; ironically, out of all the created order, only humans seem to have forgotten them. There is also a center-point of the Dance, and a central Dancer.

THE DANCING FOOL

In addition to the deck of ur-tarot cards, Williams' *The Greater Trumps* introduces us to a set of gold figurines placed on a very peculiar table, the top of which was

> ...hidden, for it was covered by a plate of what looked like gold, marked very intricately with a pattern, or perhaps with two patterns, one of squares, and one of circles, so that the eyes, as with a chessboard, saw now one and now the other as predominant. Upon that plate of gold were a number of little figures, each about three inches high, also of gold, it seemed, very wonderfully wrought; so that the likeness to the chessboard was even more pronounced, for to any hasty spectator (could such a one ever have penetrated there) the figures might have seemed like those in a game; only there were many of them, and they were all in movement. Gently and continuously they went, immingling, unresting—as if to some complicated measure, and as if of their own volition. There must have been nearly a hundred of them, and from the golden plate upon which they went came a slight sound of music—more like an echo than a sound—sometimes quickening, sometimes slowing, to which the golden figures kept a duteous rhythm, or perhaps the faint sound itself was but their harmonized movement upon their field.[11]

Each of the figurines is a statuette depicting one of the tarot cards. Both the cards and the figurines represent the Dance, and had originally been made together. Somehow, however, they had been separated and the gypsies believed the cards to be lost. Henry and his grandfather Aaron Lee are excited by the rediscovery of the cards, and believe that if the two can be brought together again, they would be able to control the forces each figure represents. They would be able to "direct" the Dance, in other words—a power any magician would envy.

The only figure not moving on the table is the Fool, corresponding to the "0" card of the tarot's greater trumps. It sits motionless in the center of the table while all the other figurines whirl about it, seemingly under their own power (or the power of an unseen Other). At first, Sybil can't see the figure of the Fool, but later she is able to see that, instead of being motionless, it was in fact moving, interacting with the other figures, but so quickly that no eye but hers could detect its movements.

Later, as Love does its work in Nancy, she too is able to discern the Fool's movement:

> She knew where the golden light came from among the images; it came from the figure of the Fool who moved so much the most swiftly, who seemed to be everywhere at once, whose irradiation shone therefore so universally upward that it maintained the circle of gold high over all, under which the many other rays of colour mingled and were dominated now by one, now by another.[12]

This aspect of the Fool is reminiscent of Krishna in the myth of the Rasa Dance, in which we learn about a group of cowgirls who snuck out at night to dance with Krishna, and each experienced him dancing with her alone.[13]

In *The Greater Trumps*, Christ is the fool, the still center and fiery sun around which everything else in the universe revolves. The Fool represents Christ both in his ubiquity (Eph 4:10) and in the nature of God's wisdom, which seems like foolishness to the world. As St. Paul explained to the Christians in Corinth,

> For the message about the cross is foolishness to those who are perishing, but to us who are being saved it is the power of God... For since, in the wisdom of God, the world did not know God through wisdom, God decided, through the foolishness of the proclamation, to save those who believe. For Jews ask for signs and Greeks desire wisdom, but we proclaim Christ crucified, a stumbling block to Jews and foolishness to gentiles, but to those who are the called, both Jews and Greeks, Christ the power of God and the wisdom of God. For God's foolishness is wiser than human wisdom, and God's weakness is stronger than human strength.[14]

Williams seems to be directly referencing this passage when he writes,

> There was to be a time, the legends said, when one should arise who should understand the mystery of the cards and the images, and by due subjection in victory and victory in subjection should come to a secret beyond all, which secret—it had always been supposed by those few who had looked on the shapes, and few they had been even over the centuries—had itself to do with the rigid figure of the Fool.[15]

The Fool only seems rigid (unmoving) to those who do not have "eyes to see." Those like Sybil and Nancy, however, who can see the Fool ministering to all the images simultaneously, understand this mystery, because they have come to know the one "through whom all things were made" (Jn 1:3), who "is before all things," in whom "all things hold together" (Col 1:17), and who, "though he existed in the form of God, did not regard equality with God as something to be grasped, but emptied himself, taking the form of a slave, assuming human likeness" (Phil 2:6–7). Once more, we are confronted with the foolishness of the Gospel, for evil cannot understand why anyone would pour oneself out for another. Williams holds forth on this idea in "The Redeemed City":

> It was uttered as a mockery by the incredulous when they saw the City in its agony; they said: 'Others He saved; Himself He could not save.' It was irony, but the Gospel is beyond irony; its affirmations are so literal that they are bound to seem ironical to the foolish, and the ironies of the foolish are discovered to be its own most precise definitions. He who could not save Himself saved others, and required that we should be one with Him in that, as in all.[16]

For Cockburn, this image of Christ as the Fool seems to have been particularly powerful, for he shows up in many songs from this period. As early as 1978, likely very soon after he read *The Greater Trumps*, he sings,

It's time for the singers of songs without hope
to take a hard look and start from scratch again.
It's time for these headlights racing
against inescapable dark to be just forgotten.
It's time for Harlequin to leap out of the future
into the midst of a world of dancers.
It's time for us all to stand hushed
in the cathedral of silence waiting at the river's end.[17]

In his autobiography, Cockburn acknowledges that he wrote this song after reading Harvey Cox's *The Feast of Fools*,[18] but it is hard to see "It's time for Harlequin to leap out of the future into the midst of a world of dancers" as anything but an allusion (conscious or not) to the Fool amid the Dance as depicted in *The Greater Trumps*. But it also recalls a line from "The Founding of the Company" in Williams' *The Region of the Summer Stars*:

> To neighbour

whom and as the Omnipotence wills is a fetch
of grace; the lowest wretch is called greatest
—and may be—on the feast of fools. The God-bearer
is the prime and sublime image of entire superfluity.[19]

But it was on Cockburn's next album that the Dancing Fool would really take center stage. In the opening song of 1979's *Dancing in the Dragon's Jaws*, Cockburn paints a picture of Christ singing and dancing the world into being, reminiscent of both Nataraja (Sanskrit for "Lord of the Dance," the image of Shiva dancing the universe in his hoop of flame) and Aslan singing the creation of Narnia in *The Magician's Nephew*:

Centred on silence, counting on nothing,
I saw you standing on the sea.
And everything was dark except for
sparks the wind struck from your hair;
sparks that turned to wings around you,
angel voices mixed with seabird cries,
fields of motion, surging outward,
questions that contain their own replies...

You were dancing, I saw you dancing,
throwing your arms toward the sky.
Fingers opening like flares,
stars were shooting everywhere.
Lines of power bursting outward
along the channels of your song.
Mercury waves flashed under your feet,
shots of silver in the shell-pink dawn...[20]

This vision of the (singing and sung) Word bringing all things into being is not just a sublime portrayal of Johannine Christology, it ranks with any of the mythopoeic theophanies spun by the Inklings themselves.

In the very next song on that same album, the Dancing Fool shows up again, this time embodying many of Williams' themes discussed above, including the Fool's ministry to all the tarot figures at once, Nancy's "circle of gold," and a juxtaposition of the "wisdom of the world" with the foolishness of the Gospel:

Women and men moved back and forth
in between effect and cause.
And just beyond the range of normal sight,
this glittering joker was dancing in the dragon's jaws.

Let me be a little of your breath,
moving over the face of the deep.
I want to be a particle of your light,
flowing over the hills of morning.

The only sign you gave of who you were,
when you first came walking down the road,
was the way the dust motes danced around
your feet in a cloud of gold.

But everything you see's not the way it seems—
tears can sing and joy shed tears.
You can take the wisdom of this world
and give it to the ones who think it all ends here.[21]

The "glittering joker...dancing in the dragon's jaws" is a striking image, recalling Gregory of Nyssa's "fishhook" theory of the atonement, which pictured Satan as Leviathan, swallowing the "bait" of the crucified Christ (whereupon Christ, having gained entrance to hell, proceeded to destroy it and liberate its captives).[22]

In yet another example from that album, Cockburn gives us a song in French featuring several images of nature, each brimming with wonder. He finishes the song by pointing to their source:

Un rire sonne comme le cristal
Dans le ciel vide —
Quelqu'un danse comme une flamme![23]

[translation]
A laugh rings like crystal
in the empty sky —
someone is dancing like a flame!

Three guesses who that might be...

A couple of albums later, the image of the Dancing Fool standing motionless in the center appears in the context of a Native American ritual. Cockburn's stacked images are doing a lot here: making a comparison between the "first Adam" and the "second Adam,"[24] and connecting the identity of the "original man" with creation itself. Cockburn has long been an advocate for Native rights in his home country of Canada, and has sung about Native issues frequently. In this song, he reminds us that while so-called "civilized" people have forgotten the Dance, native peoples have not—they too are the fool at the center of the Dance, not seeming to move, not needing to change (i.e., be "colonized" or "civilized"), not needing to be anything but what they are.

First man, last man, dancing man, man dancing,
hoops in hand, trampled grass, circle spreading,
voices flame above crazy coyote heartbeat drum.

I see sunrise on the plains, big river at dusk
perpetual pillar of dust on prairie rim, and always overhead
those wings—circling, turning.

He's the earth, he's the egg, he's the eagle, always circling,
always turning—always comes back to the centre.[25]

In both Williams and Cockburn, the Dancing Fool represents

the original dancer, who instructs us in the Dance, leads the Dance, and is himself a personification of the Dance. He is omnipresent, dancing with every creature simultaneously, and somehow always also the centrepoint of the Dance. As God, he is the circle dance "whose center is everywhere and whose circumference is nowhere."[26]

---

1. Miller, 6–7.
2. Plato, *Timaeus*, 40.
3. Miller, 56.
4. *Ibid.*, 60–61.
5. Acts of John 95, quoted in Miller, 82.
6. In the Greek, περί = around; χορός = dance or movement.
7. *Beyond Personality,* 21–22; quoted in Barber, *Patterns,* 35.
8. *GT,* 15.
9. *Ibid.,* 88–89.
10. "Everywhere Dance," *YNSE.*
11. *GT,* 22–23.
12. *GT,* 131.
13. Vishnu Purana, Part 5, Chapter 13.
14. 1 Cor. 1:18, 21–25.
15. *GT,* 149.
16. "The Redeemed City," *Image of the City*, 107.
17. "Feast of Fools," *FAO.*
18. *Cockburn*, 160.
19. "The Founding of the Company," *Region of the Summer Stars,* 159.
20. "Creation Dream," *DDJ.*
21. "Hills of Morning," *DDJ.*
22. "...in order to secure that the ransom in our behalf might be easily accepted by him who required it, the Deity was hidden under the veil of our nature, that so, as with ravenous fish, the hook of the Deity might be gulped down along with the bait of flesh, and thus, life being introduced into the house of death." Gregory of Nyssa, *The Great Catechism*, ed. by Phillip Schaff and Henry Wace (Oxford: Parker and Company, 1893), chap. 24.
23. "Badlands Flashback," *DDJ.*
24. 1 Cor. 15:45.
25. "Hoop Dancer" *TWN.*
26. This saying is attributed to various sources, including Empedocles, Hermes Trismegistus, St. Bonaventure, Nicholas of Cusa, and Voltaire.

10

THE IMAGE OF THE ROSE

In *The Figure of Beatrice*, Williams writes, "Hell is a funnel, Heaven a rose."[1] He is, of course, talking about Dante's depiction of both in his *Divine Comedy*. In Canto 31 of the *Paradiso*, the great poet attempts to describe the ineffable glories of heaven:

> So now, displayed before me as a rose
> Of snow-white purity, the sacred might
> I saw, whom with His blood Christ made His spouse...
>
> Down floating to the Flower, from row to row,
> Each [angel] ministered the peace and burning love
> They gathered in their wafting to and fro.
>
> Between the Flower and that which blazed above
> The volant concourse interposed no screen
> To dim the splendor and the sight thereof
>
> For God's rays penetrate with shafts so keen
> Through all the universe, in due degree,
> There's naught can parry them or intervene.[2]

In their commentary, Dorothy Sayers and Barbara Reynolds reveal the meaning behind the image of this rose:

> The circle of light, which is the light of God's glory, forms the yellow of the vast white rose which Dante next beholds. Its petals rising in more than a thousand tiers are the thrones of the blessed, whom Dante can perceive despite the distance, for he is now beyond the limitations of time and space. The rose in mediaeval literature was the symbol of earthly love; Dante's white rose is the symbol of divine love.[3]

In *All Hallows' Eve*, Williams makes repeated allusion to this mystic rose of Dante's heaven. It is certain that it is no accident and quite conscious, as there are 52 occurrences of the word "rose" in *All Hallows' Eve*, while in his previous novel, *Descent into Hell*, there are only 27. Even the verb form of "rose" is invoked out of proportion, indicating that Williams was not above a good pun when it suited him.

The Rose represents not just the heaven of our eventual destination, but also the spiritual development of the soul on its journey there. As Williams writes, "Thus a man's own proper perfection has been, as it were, acquired in Youth; now he is concerned with a wider, and therefore a greater, perfection. 'Man,' Dante quotes here from Aristotle, 'is a civic animal,' but Aristotle's phrase is quickened and illuminated by Dante's. The man of nobility now is 'like a rose opening.'"[4]

In *All Hallows' Eve*, we see the budding of this rose in Lester, as she makes choices that benefit others rather than herself. As we watch her moral development, her movement toward Love, the Rose (as above, so below) colors the scene with itself. When the villain, magician Simon LeClerk, exploits his daughter Betty (a magical Moonchild of his own making), forcing her to go into a visionary state to visit the future and report on what she sees, he does not know that the ghost of Lester is also present:

> Because it would have been, and was, so unimportant, he did not see in the pale and exhausted girl in the bed any of the sudden runnels of roseal light which Lester now saw, as if the blood itself were changed and richly glowing through the weary flesh.[5]

Later in the novel, she sees the same glow, but this time it pervades the City:

> Not only space but time spread out around her as she went. She saw a glowing and glimmering City, of which the life was visible as a roseal wonder within.[6]

Williams has a tendency to stack his metaphors until his prose becomes top-heavy and unwieldy, and *All Hallows' Eve* is no exception. In the novel's climax a fierce rainstorm erupts, symbolizing baptism and the assumption of Creation into Godself:

> Within the rain a fresher light was opening. It shone on the rain and on the river; and the room with its companies was still there, but it stood on the river, which flowed through it, and in the rain, which fell through it. The light was like dawn, except that it had in it a tinge redder than dawn, and the same tinge was in the river and the rain, exquisite and blood-roseal, delicate and enriching... Above her the sky every moment grew more high and empty; the rain fell from a source far beyond all clouds.[7]

In the aftermath of this rain, Lester sees a mass of her fellow ghosts, those who did not move toward Love, being ushered by the glow—as if it were some vast, heavenly hand—toward their chosen fate:

> The great-headed, great-cloaked, steadily walking forms were wholly unlike her, but yet they were she—double, immense,

> concealed, walking through the unfelt rain on the unyielding water, antipathetic, relegated to antipathy; as if in the shadowy City of her early death she had gone another way. Behind them, as they went, the faint roseal glow in the waters and the rain gathered thicker and followed, and deepened as it followed. The colour of it—rose or blood or fire—struck up the descending lines of rain and was lost somewhere in that empty upper sky above her; but below it was by now almost a wall which moved after those forms, and absorbed and changed the antipathy they diffused; and all behind them the freshness of the waters and the light was free and lovely.

Father Simon also watches this procession, and feels his power weakening with every step:

> The grace drove against them from behind, as if it were driving them back to him; or perhaps it had been their coming which stirred and shook the unseen clouds, and left a void the living waters rushed in to fill. The roseal glow behind them in the waters was now very deep and filled the window with what was becoming not so much a glow as a fume of colour... He managed to pronounce a word of command. They stopped, but then also he too stopped. He obeyed himself. He knew he needed time—time and shelter from the rain and the rose-light, and the rose-smell; which was not only a rose-smell but a smell of blood and of burning, of all those great crimson things... He hated them, and since they held his hate they hated him. The hate seemed to swell in a nightmare bubble within the rose which was forming round them, cloud in cloud, overlying like petals. Simon made a quick half-spring as if to overleap it, and so did they; but he failed and fell back, and so did they. The smell of the rose was changing to the smell of his last act, to the smell of blood. He looked down; he saw below him the depth of the rose... The rose began to withdraw. He felt himself carried with

> it, and slipping more deeply into it. The smell of blood was in his nostrils; the touch of burning on his flesh; this was what the crimson must be to him. He stared, as he sank and as that in which he was held moved in its own fashion, at the rain of swift-darting points between him and himself... He stared at them, imbecile; imbecile, they stared back—farther and farther, deeper and deeper, through the rose and the burning and the blood.[8]

Simon's experience here recalls the Eastern Orthodox belief that all souls have the same destination—the unmediated presence of God. But while those who are acquainted with God find that presence blissful, those who have denied that acquaintance find the very same presence caustic.[9] The Rose is the Rose, it welcomes all, to Simon's horror.

By now it will come as no surprise that rose imagery shows up in Cockburn's work as well. In his 1980 song from his album *Humans*, "The Rose Above the Sky," he sings:

Something jeweled slips away
'round the next bend with a splash.
Laughing at the hands I hold out,
only air within their grasp...

Gutless arrogance and rage
burn apart the best of tries.
You carry the weight of inherited sorrow
from your first day 'til you die,
toward that hilltop where the road
forever becomes one with the sky

'til the Rose above the sky
opens
and the light behind the sun
takes all.

Cockburn has said in an interview that the song is "about moving from downness into something that opens up, although what that something *is* is not really spelled out."[10] Perhaps that is true only within the context of the song, but in relation to Williams' work, there is a lot to unpack in these lines. Pointing pithily to the brokenness of the human condition, tipping his hat to the reality of original sin, Cockburn suggests that every life is moving toward its own Golgotha, "that hilltop where the road / forever becomes one with the sky." This is reminiscent of Battle Hill in *Descent into Hell*, another image of the place where the transcendent and the imminent converge in the ultimate sacrificial Symbol. The torpor of the verse gives way to a victorious, strident beat in the chorus, and Dante's Rose receives all that is flowing toward it, without discrimination, just as the Mundaka Upanishad says all rivers find their end in the ocean.[11]

That analogy must have occurred to Cockburn too, since in the next verse he sings,

Ozone on the midnight wind
got me thinking of the sea,
and the mercies of the currents that brought
me to you and you to me.
And in the silence at the heart of things
where all true meetings come to be

I see the Rose above the sky
open
and the light behind the sun
takes all.

Astronomical floral imagery surfaces as well in Cockburn's 1986 song, "Lily of the Midnight Sky" from his album *World of Wonders*:

Soldiers of sunrise—shooting into a forest of flowers.

Slow motion
petals float into pink crimson white,
grow wings,
flutter into mountainous distance,
flutter like a stadium full of applauding hands.
I raise a fist to the marauding sun that has hidden you away...

Nobody else could be you.
If only I could see you.
I should be able to touch you somehow.
I can reach you if I try
Lily of the midnight sky.

The flowers he sees in a Colorado forest point him toward a transcendent symbol of resurrection and Life. But it is not salvation that Cockburn wrestles with here—it is abandonment, specifically divine abandonment, what Luther called *Deus absconditus* ("the hidden God"). In the first verse of the song, he names the problem directly:

The cold of your absence blows from
the silent TV, the parking lot,
the balcony with clothes waving good-bye/hello...

In the final chorus, he expresses his desperation for divine communion in terms that rival "*Eli, Eli, lama sabachthani*" in their poignancy:

While you look from on high,
spare a smile as I
put on my dog mask and howl for you.
I can reach you if I try
Lily of the midnight sky.

Cockburn invokes the image of the rose again in "Southland

of the Heart," Cockburn's imaginative setting of the 23rd Psalm, where once more the rose represents a transcendent hope that is just out of reach:

When they've taken all your money
and then come back for your clothes.
When your hands are full of thorns
but you can't quit groping for the rose.

In the southland of the heart,
where night blooms perfume the breeze,
lie down,
take your rest with me.[12]

Just as Williams employed imagery colored with a "roseal" glow to indicate something affected, infiltrated, or penetrated by the Transcendence, Cockburn has done the same. On 1979's "After the Rain," he sings,

After the rain in the streets light flows like blood
I can just taste salt on the humid wind.[13]

And again, on 2001's "Messenger Wind:"

In a horse-powered sleigh at the top of the town,
sun coming up paints the snow all around with rose light...

To be one more voice in the human choir,
rising like smoke from the mystical fire of the heart...

Sun coming up paints the snow all around,
rose on the roofs and the trees and the ground,
and the stream.
In my dream,
messenger wind swooping out of the sky

lights each tiny speck in my human kaleidoscope
with hope.[14]

Cockburn invokes the rose-colored atmosphere once more on "States I'm In":

Seen rose gold haze at the end of the day,
ragged-winged hawk swooping down on prey,
curtain going up on the night time shadow play.[15]

Writing about the song, Cockburn explains, "It's literally a 'dark night of the soul' kind of song, as it starts with sunset and ends with dawn. It passes through the night. The song is about illusion and self-delusion, looking at the tricks you play on yourself."[16] The "rose gold haze" at the end of the day is evocative of order, safety, productivity, connection, while the "night time shadow play," evokes disintegration, disconnection, and danger. Like Williams, Cockburn is a reluctant optimist, not letting go of hope, but not willing to look away from the darkness and dis-ease of contemporary life, either.

---

1. *Figure of Beatrice*, 225.
2. Dante, Canto XXXI, lines 1-3, 16–24.
3. *Ibid.*, from the commentary on Canto XXX, 324.
4. *Beatrice*, 81.
5. *AHE*, 133–134.
6. *Ibid.*, 163.
7. *Ibid.*, 223.
8. *Ibid.*, 229–232.
9. "Love will enrobe everything with its sacred Fire which will flow like a river from the throne of God and will irrigate paradise. But this same river of Love —for those who have hate in their hearts—will suffocate and burn." — Alexandre Kalomiros, "The River of Fire," [presentation] 1980 Orthodox Conference, Seattle, WA, 1980; http://blogs.ancientfaith.com/glory2godforallthings/the-river-of-fire-kalomiros/
10. "Bruce Cockburn's Quiet Optimism," *High Fidelity*, 1981, by Stephen Holden.
11. Mundaka Upanishad, 2:2:8.

12. "Southland of the Heart," *D2H*.
13. "After the Rain," *DDJ*.
14. "Messenger Wind," *YNSE*.
15. "States I'm In," *BoB*.
16. Taken from the *Bone On Bone* press release.

11
THE IMAGE OF THE STREAM

The last image we will consider goes by a variety of names—where Williams uses "flow" and "channels," Cockburn prefers the more concrete (and poetic) image of a stream. But regardless of the name, the action is the same—all things are moving toward their restoration in God, and this river cannot be diverted or dammed. Williams sees the force behind this current as Divine. He writes, "The Holy Ghost, it is declared, drives us towards a union with that Union. What He created, we must choose—accepting in the Re-creation the original creation."[1] Furthermore, this divine impulse toward Union is relentless. Williams once told a friend, the "re-union of man and God is pursued everywhere and at all times, from which nothing is alien and to which all things are directed."[2] In *The Figure of Beatrice*, he describes this more poetically: "...all the images are moving sweetly and strongly into God."[3] In the novels, he calls this movement "flow." This movement is present even in his earliest novel, *Shadows of Ecstasy*, where he writes,

> As [Roger] made ready for sleep he thought once more of Isabel...They did not answer each other; they flowed towards each other and intermingled, and dissolved each into others,

> meaning in sound, sound in meaning, and always fresh ripples rose and ran on that dark surface, away towards the bounded infinity, and in and between them all was the vast power of which they were but gleaming movement momently seen. Between them, as into that vast, received and to be strengthened, he sank to sleep.[4]

The movement is likewise present in his last novel, *All Hallows' Eve*:

> The river flowed steadily on...the Thames was still the Thames, but within it the infinite gradations of clarity deepened to something else. That other flow sustained and carried the layers of water above it; and as Lester saw it she felt a great desire to discover its source...[5]

But it is in his 1930 novel, *War in Heaven,* that the image of flow is visited again and again:

> The Archdeacon looked, and grew serious. His spirit felt its own unreasonable gaiety opening into a wider joy; its dance became a more vital but therefore a vaster thing. Faintly again he heard the sound of music, but now not from without, or indeed from within, from some non-spatial, non-temporal, non-personal existence. It was music, but not yet music, or if music, then the music of movement itself—sound produced, not by things, but in the nature of things. He looked, and looked again, and felt himself part of a moving river flowing towards some narrow channel on a ripple of which the Graal was as a gleam of supernatural light. "Yes," he said softly, "it is the Cup."[6]

> [The Archdeacon] considered, in this, the chalice offered at every altar, and was aware again of a general movement of all things towards a narrow channel. Of all material things still discoverable in the world the Graal had been nearest to the

> Divine and Universal Heart. Sky and sea and land were moving, not towards that vessel, but towards all it symbolized and had held.[7]
>
> But the Graal stood like any other chalice, as dull as the furniture about it. Only the Archdeacon, and he much more faintly, was conscious of that steady movement of creation flowing towards and through the narrow channel of its destiny.[8]

This image of nature flowing toward the Graal is referenced by Cockburn explicitly in his song, "No Footprints," when he sings,

Mist hangs above hills,
above mist hangs stone face of mountain.
Above mountain face hangs a net of sky —
crack! There are wings and they rip the net!
And the dance flows on,
everything flows toward the rim of that
shining cup.[9]

There is much to unpack in this brief verse—beginning with the ripping of the net (the web, the Whole), which evokes the image of the Net of Indra, an image of oneness and interpenetration common to both Hindu and Mahayana Buddhist scriptures.[10] But no sooner is the creation rent than the restoration is begun as "the dance flows on," and "everything flows toward the rim of that shining cup."

This may be the only song in which the Graal and "flow" are mentioned together, but there is no shortage of "flow" imagery in Cockburn's lyrics, as it shows up in abundance, and often in salvific context:

When the angel shouts from the heart of the sun,
and the living water flows down,

can I go with you?[11]

Let me be a little of your breath,
moving over the face of the deep —
I want to be a particle of your light
flowing over the hills of morning.[12]

Water of life is going to flow again,
changed from the blood of heroes and knaves.
The word mercy's going to have a new meaning
when we are judged by the children of our slaves.[13]

This current flows between us,
that will not be denied.
You draw me in towards you,
like the moon pulls at the tide.[14]

Don't tell me there is no Mystery,
it overflows my cup.[15]

Likewise, all of the examples from *War in Heaven* noted above mention the image of the "narrow channel" through which this flow travels. As Gwendolen Grant notes, "The imagery of the 'narrow channel' is repeated throughout the story, imitating the shape of the cup as all things pour towards and through it. The Archdeacon can see past the Graal's physical existence, gaining a glimpse of its true nature in this channel."[16] And what is it that flows through that channel? Ann Ridler says it is grace: "...by our own intention of good will we may make ourselves a channel for God's grace to flow towards another soul."[17]

Cockburn also makes use of this "channel" image. In "Creation Dream," he sings,

Lines of power
bursting outward

along the channels of your song.[18]

In another song from the same album, his use is strangely tender and technical at the same time:

Through these channels/words
I want to touch you,
touch you deep down
where you live;
not for power but
because I love you.[19]

The way Williams understands this flow is similar to how "divine energies" are defined by late Byzantine theologian Gregory Palamas (1296–1357) and as found in Orthodox Christian teaching since. He taught that while God's essence was unknowable (a staple of the Via Negativa), God's "uncreated energies" can be experienced through the ways God shows up in the world, the sensually perceivable "effects" of God's action and presence. As Christoph Schneider explains,

> [Palamas] points out that the divine essence and energy are not identical and (following Dionysius the Areopagite) a distinction must be drawn between the imparticipable (*amethekton*) which is the divine essence, the participable (*methekton*) which is the divine energy, and that which participates (*metechon*), which is created beings. The divine energies mediate between the one uncreated divine essence and the plurality of created participating beings.[20]

The flow itself seems to refer more to an action than a thing—perhaps the action of these divine energies—while the channel seems to signify the immediate means, the physical container through which the flow pours out (such as a chalice, a sacrament, or a living person). But what is important in Williams (and in

Cockburn) is the effect of this flow—bringing good out of evil by knitting back together that which has been torn.

---

1. "The Redeemed City," *Image of the City*, 104.
2. Charles Williams to Phyllis Jones, Jan 1929, Bodleian MS Res. c. 320/I, letter 34, qtd. in Lindop, *3rd Inkling*, 153.
3. *Figure of Beatrice*, 97.
4. *SoE*, 167–168.
5. *AHE*, 190.
6. *WiH*, 112.
7. *Ibid.*, 132.
8. *Ibid.*, 175.
9. "No Footprints," *DDJ*.
10. *Atharva Veda* 8.8.6-8; *Buddhāvataṃsaka Sutra*, book 30.
11. "Can I Go With You?" *FAO*.
12. "Hills of Morning," *DDJ*.
13. "Broken Wheel," *ICF*.
14. "Someone I Used to Love," *D2H*.
15. "Mystery," *LSCN*.
16. Grant, x.
17. Ridler, xlix.
18. "Creation Dream," *DDJ*.
19. "No Footprints," *DDJ*.
20. Christoph Schneider. "Divine Energies," from *St. Andrew's Encyclopedia of Theology*, referencing *Triads* III.2.25.

EPILOGUE

It is not surprising that another artist would pick up Williams' baton and carry on his ideas, but one might expect it to be another novelist, perhaps producing pastiches after the fashion of *That Hideous Strength*. But any lesser writer than Lewis would have a hard time being taken seriously (or even getting noticed, given Williams' relative obscurity). It makes sense that an artist working in another medium altogether would be more successful—and what form more fitting than poetry/song lyrics?

Of course, *That Hideous Strength* is not wholesale pastiche—Lewis certainly captured the mood of Williams' novels, and Williams' ideas were deeply influential on Lewis' thought and writing, but Lewis knew his own mind, and as much as he intended to honor his friend, he also took the novel in a direction that Williams would not have.

Likewise, Cockburn, influenced as he is by Williams, has taken his art to places Williams would not have recognized—from the betrayal of native peoples to the slaughter of innocents in Central America. They come from different national, social, and generational cultures. Cockburn, a Baby Boomer, brings his generation's idealism, passion, and issues to his art, making it a very different thing from the concerns of someone from the Lost Generation, as Williams was. Both are cynics, but the seats of their cynicisms have a different location. Both are introverts, yet Cockburn has chosen to make his life more of an open book.

Yet, as I hope is clear by now, the influence of Williams' ideas and images on Cockburn's art has been profound. I can think of no other artist, working in any medium, who has so consistently and successfully advanced Williams' project.

In an interview, Cockburn said, "Although I want to be taken seriously, some people take it too far and start investing my insights with greater power than they ought to. At that point, you have to chuckle. It's great for other people to take you seriously, but you'd better not be guilty of doing it to yourself."[1]

I am sure that there are those who will dismiss some of the connections drawn in this book as "taking it too far," simply the product of my own projections. I am open to such feedback and will own what I can. I'm certain I have not been right about everything I've said, as I have not known either man or the deepest contents of their hearts beyond what they have chosen to reveal.

I did meet Bruce once, after a show. After lamely attempting to describe what his songs meant to me, I broke down in a blubbering pile of goo. He put his hand on my shoulder and said, "Sometimes, the human touch..." and then he hugged me. It was an incomplete sentence, but it was all that needed to be said.

These two men have been the most important influences on my own life—spiritually and artistically. I call *All Hallows' Eve* "the shout that started the avalanche that brought me here." I made a vow before Williams' grave to bring all of his writings that I could back into print—a promise I have kept. And Bruce has been on my turntable more than any other singer-songwriter. I wonder if I would be a Christian today had it not been that, at a certain point in my life, I could not dismiss Christianity outright for the simple reason that Cockburn was a Christian. So there must be something there, right?

Until I started this project, I considered it a bit of an accident that Cockburn had even heard of Williams. Then I started mapping the connections, a process that took me more deeply into both of their creative worlds. As the connections revealed themselves, I realized it was no coincidence that these two men exerted such a powerful pull on my life—they were often saying the same things, things that my soul thirsted for desperately.

I think there are others who thirst for these ideas and images, too. They are, after all, simply creative framings of the Gospel—the Good News of the Incarnation, of Ubiquity and Theosis, of the desperate and relentless Love of God. Both are skilled at getting past our "watchful dragons," as Lewis put it—Williams through potboiling occult thrillers and Cockburn through catchy folk (and, later, rock) music. To revisit T.S. Eliot's letter to Williams, "One of your most important functions in life is to instill sound doctrine into people...without their knowing it... This is not a matter of Gilding the Pill, but of introducing the maximum amount of Physic into the treacle."[2] But to reduce the work of these artists to craven, manipulative means of proselytization misrepresents them. Both were and are, in their art, simply trying to tell the Truth—about their lives, their mystical experiences, and their lived experience of God. They are not islands—as none of us are—but absorbed ideas and images that spoke to them, and then continued to let them speak. They are—as all of us are—co-inherent.

---

1. Boehm.
2. T.S. Eliot to Charles Williams, 14 December 1940, Bodleian Ms. Res. c.137, f.2., quoted in Roukema, *viii*.

WORKS CITED

WORKS BY CHARLES WILLIAMS

All Hallows' Eve (London: Faber & Faber, 1945; Hannacroix, NY: Apocryphile Press, 2021; includes a new introduction by Edward Gauntlett).

Collected Plays by Charles Williams. John Heath-Stubbs, ed (London: Oxford University Press, 1963)

Descent into Hell (London: Victor Gollancz, 1933; Hannacroix, NY: Apocryphile Press, 2021; includes a new introduction by Grevel Lindop).

Descent of the Dove, The (London: Longman's, 1939)

Divorce (London: Oxford University Press, 1920)

Figure of Beatrice, The (London: Faber & Faber, 1943)

Greater Trumps, The (London: Victor Gollancz, 1932; Hannacroix, NY: Apocryphile Press, 2022; includes a new introduction by Sørina Higgins)

He Came Down from Heaven (London: Heinemann, 1938. Edition cited: *He Came Down from Heaven* and *The Forgiveness of Sins*; Hannacroix, NY: Apocryphile Press, 2005)

Image of the City and Other Essays, The. Anne Ridler, ed. (London: Oxford University Press, 1958)

Outlines of Romantic Theology. Alice Hadfield, ed. (Grand Rapids, MI: Eerdman's, 1990)

Place of the Lion, The (London: Mundanus, 1931; Hannacroix, NY: Apocryphile Press, 2022; includes a new introduction by Grevel Lindop)

Region of the Summer Stars, The (London: Oxford University Press, 1944). Edition cited is included in *Taliessin through Logres / The Region of the Summer Stars / Arthurian Torso* (Grand Rapids: Eerdmans, 1974)

Religion and Love in Dante: The Theology of Romantic Love (Westminster: Dacre Press, 1941)

Shadows of Ecstasy (London: Faber & Faber, 1937; Hannacroix, NY: Apocryphile Press, 2022; includes a new introduction by Aren Roukema)

Silver Stair, The (London: Herbert and Daniel, 1912)

Taliessin Through Logres (London: Oxford University Press, 1938). Edition cited is included in *Taliessin through Logres / The Region of the Summer Stars / Arthurian Torso* (Grand Rapids: Eerdmans, 1974)

Windows of Night: Poems (London: Oxford University Press, 1924)

Witchcraft (London: Faber & Faber, 1941)

OTHER WORKS CITED

Arthurian Torso. "Williams and the Arthuriad" by Lewis, C.S. (London: Oxford University Press, 1948). Edition cited is included in *Taliessin through Logres / The Region of the Summer Stars / Arthurian Torso* (Grand Rapids: Eerdmans, 1974)

Ashenden, Gavin. *Alchemy & Integration* (Kent, OH: Kent University Press, 2008)

Barber, *Celian.* Stephen Barber. *Celian Moment, The* (UK: Greystone Press, 2017; Hannacroix, NY: Apocryphile Press, 2024)

Barber, *Patterns.Patterns of Glory.* Steven Barber (Hannacroix, NY: Apocryphile Press, 2024)

Beyond Personality: The Christian Idea of God. Lewis, C.S. (New York: Macmillan, 1945)

Boehm, Mike. "Bruce Cockburn: Interior Motive", *Los Angeles Times,* 22 November 1994.

Carpenter, Humphrey. *The Inklings: C.S. Lewis, J.R.R. Tolkien, Charles Williams and Their Friends* (Boston: Houghton Mifflin Co., 1979)

Cavaliero, Glen. *Charles Williams, Poet of Theology* (Grand Rapids: Eerdman's, 1983)

Cockburn, Bruce. *Rumours of Glory: A Memoir* (NY: HarperCollins, 2014)

Dante, *The Divine Comedy III: Paradise*, trans. by Dorothy Sayers and Barbara Reynolds (NY: Penguin Books, 1962, 2004)

Eckhart, John. *Meditations with Meister Eckhart.* Fox, Matthew, ed. (Santa Fe: Bear & Co., 1983)

Essays. Essays Presented to Charles Williams. Lewis, C.S., ed (London: Oxford University Press, 1947)

Grant, Gwendolen. "Introduction" to *War in Heaven* (Hannacroix, NY: Apocryphile Press, 2021)

Gunnar, Urang. *Shadows of Heaven* (London: SCM Press, 1971)

Hadfield, Alice. "Introduction" to *Outlines of Romantic Theology* (Grand Rapids, MI: Eerdman's, 1990)

Howard, Thomas. *The Novels of Charles Williams* (London: Oxford University Press, 1983)

Lindop, *DiH.* Lindop, Grevel. "Introduction" to *Descent into Hell* (Hannacroix, NY: Apocryphile Press, 2022)

Lindop, *PoL.* Lindop, Grevel. "Introduction to *Place of the Lion, The* (Hannacroix, NY: Apocryphile Press, 2022)

Lindop, *3rd Inkling. Charles Williams: The Third Inkling* (Oxford: Oxford University Press, 2015)

McKnight, Scott. *A Community Called Atonement* (Nashville, TN: Abingdon Press, 2007)

Miller, James. *Measures of Wisdom: The Cosmic Dance in Classical and Christian Antiquity* (Toronto: University of Toronto Press, 1986)

Newman, Barbara. "Charles Williams and the Companions of the Co-inherence," *Spiritus*, Vol. 9, issue 1; Spring, 2009)

Peura, Simo. "What God Gives Man Receives: Luther on Salvation." *Union with Christ,* ed. by Carl E. Braaten and Robert W. Jenson (Grand Rapids: Eerdmans, 1998)

Ridler, Anne. "Introduction" to Williams' *The Image of the City* (London: Oxford University Press, 1958)

Roukema, Aren. "Introduction" to *Shadows of Ecstasy* (Hannacroix, NY: Apocryphile Press, 2022)

Shideler, Mary M. *The Theology of Romantic Love: A Study in the Writings of Charles Williams* (New York: Harper & Row, 1962)

Tolkien, J.R.R. "On Fairy Stories," from *Essays Presented to Charles Williams*, C.S. Lewis, ed. (London: Oxford University Press, 1947. Edition cited: Grand Rapids, MI: Eerdman's, 1968)

ALSO BY JOHN R. MABRY

NON-FICTION
{ writing as John R. Mabry }

Soul Journeys: Christian Spirituality and Shamanism as Pathways for Wholeness and Understanding
(with co-authors Daniel L. Prechtel & Katrina Leathers)

Starting Spiritual Direction: A Guide to Getting Ready, Feeling Safe, and Getting the Most Out of Your Sessions

Spiritual Guidance Across Religions: A Sourcebook for Spiritual Directors and other People Providing Counsel to People of Differing Faith Traditions

Faithful Generations: Ministry for the Five Generations Alive Today

Growing Into God: A Beginner's Guide to Christian Mysticism

Sermons that Connect: A Beginner's Guide to Crafting and Delivering Powerful, Excellent Sermons

People of Faith: An Interfaith Companion to the Revised Common Lectionary

The Monster God: Images of Horrific Divinity in the Religions of the World

The Way of Thomas: Nine Insights for Enlightened Living from the Secret Sayings of Jesus

Noticing the Divine: Introducing Interfaith Spiritual Guidance

God Has One Eye: Mystics of the World's Religions

Faith Styles: A Spiritual Typology for Spiritual Guidance and Ministry

God As Nature Sees God: A Christian Reading of the Tao Te Ching

FICTION
{ writing as J.R. Mabry }

The Where, the Who & the What: A Gnostic Science Fiction Novel

Ash Wednesday

The Worship of Mystery

The Red Horn Saga
(with co-author Mickey Asteriou)

The Oblivion Saga
(with co-author B.J. West)

The Berkeley Blackfriars Series

Made in USA - Kendallville, IN
54486_9781965646700
03.03.2026 2019